MAN OF MERCURY

Henry St John, Viscount Bolingbroke

From an engraving by A. Millar, 1753, of a portrait by Jonathan Richardson

Man of Mercury

An Appreciation of the Mind of
Henry St John, Viscount Bolingbroke

SYDNEY WAYNE JACKMAN

With an Introduction by Sir Charles Petrie, Bart.

PALL MALL PRESS
London

OTHER BOOKS BY SYDNEY WAYNE JACKMAN

Galloping Head, Phoenix House, London, 1958
Frederick Marryat: A Diary in America, Knopf, New York, 1962
With Burgoyne from Quebec, Macmillan, Toronto, 1963
The English Reform Tradition, Prentice-Hall, Englewood Cliffs,
N.J., 1965

921
B638j

Published by PALL MALL PRESS LTD.
77-79 Charlotte Street, London W1

© 1965 Sydney Wayne Jackman

Printed in Bembo by The Garden City Press Ltd., London and
Letchworth

To
Walter Muir Whitehill

Contents

Author's Foreword

I should like to express my thanks to Edward Smith and Crane Brinton for their encouragement and support when I initially began to undertake researches in intellectual history; to Gerald Bostock for editorial assistance; to Mrs E. J. Belton the Assistant Librarian of the Forbes Library, Clare College, for invaluable aid and counsel; to the Master and Fellows of Clare College for their generous hospitality; and to the many others who answered many questions or listened patiently when approached. The publication of these essays owes much to the support of a grant from the American Philosophical Society and to that body I wish to express my appreciation. Above all, I wish to express my sincere thanks to the President and Trustees of the Rockefeller Foundation who made it possible for me to take leave from academic duties to continue my researches in eighteenth century history.

S. W. J.

Clare College, Cambridge
The University of Victoria, Victoria, British Columbia

Introduction

by

SIR CHARLES PETRIE

BART.

C.B.E. M.A. (Oxon). Hon. D.Phil. Valladolid.
F.R.Hist.S. Corresponding Member of the
Royal Spanish Academy of History. President
of the Military History Society of Ireland.

Introduction

TWO HUNDRED AND THIRTEEN years ago, on December 12, 1751, there died at the age of seventy-three Henry St John, Viscount Bolingbroke. The epitaph on his grave he wrote himself:

Here Lyes
HENRY ST. JOHN:
In the days of Queen Anne,
Secretary at War, Secretary of State, and Viscount Bolingbroke;
In the days of King George the First and King George the
Second,
Something more and better.
His attachment to Queen Anne,
Exposed him to a long and severe prosecution:
He bore it with firmness of mind.
He passed the latter part of his life at home.
The enemy of no national party,
The friend of no faction;
Distinguished under the cloud of a proscription
Which had not been entirely taken off
By zeal to maintain the Liberty
And to restore the ancient Prosperity
Of Great Britain.

After the lapse of more than two centuries it is not without interest to see how far these claims can be substantiated.

Henry St John was born at Battersea on October 1, 1678. The year of his birth was one of the most eventful in an eventful century, for it witnessed the Treaty of Nimwegen, which marked the apogee of Louis XIV, and also the revelations of Titus Oates, which ushered in a period as chaotic as any in English history. The storms raging at the time of St John's entry into the world continued to buffet it throughout his career; unless allowance is made for this fact his life will not be seen in its true perspective.

He was to become a forceful statesman of the type of Disraeli, Joseph Chamberlain and Winston Churchill; but to compare him with any of them, or even with the Younger Pitt, without taking into account the circumstances in which he was placed would be to do him a serious injustice. St John was born in and lived through not merely an era of transition, but of violent change. Twenty years before he was born there had been no king in England, only a 'Lord Protector', and on at least one occasion during his early manhood it appeared by no means improbable that another republic might be established; nevertheless in the interval he witnessed a period when the king was practically absolute. He was but ten when the Stuarts were sent into exile for the second time, yet only six years before his death the grandson of James II was at Derby at the head of a victorious army; he had been in his grave for little more than twelve months when the last Jacobite to die for his principles was executed. In effect, St John passed his life in an age of revolution, and he was the child of his age.

He came of a distinguished family, but one which had been politically much divided of late years, for whereas several members had died for Charles I, a St John had been Chief Justice of the Common Pleas under Cromwell. The future Viscount Bolingbroke was educated at Eton and possibly at Christ Church, but whether he was at Oxford or not he received a very good education. In all his writings there is to be found abundant proof of solid learning, and also of an ability to apply that learning to the problems of the day. Few English statesmen could have written *Letters on the Study and Use of History*, while in his interest in economic matters, as shown by the projected commercial treaty with France, he was in advance of his time. Throughout his works there is extensive evidence that he was deeply read in the classics, not only in Latin but also in Greek. In spite of the distractions of business and pleasure St John remained a scholar at heart. Indeed, the eloquence and erudition of his writings enables us to understand, even if we are not prepared wholly to share, the wish of the Younger Pitt, that of all the lost intellectual treasures, he would most like to see recovered a speech of St John's.

As soon as the Treaty of Ryswick, in the later months of 1697, made it possible to travel abroad once more, St John went to the continent, where he spent the greater part of two years. This expedition was no 'grand tour' as the term was understood by the fashionable young men of the day, but was undertaken for the purpose of becoming acquainted with the foreign point of view. St John went at the right age, and he was amply rewarded, as those young men always are who do as he did. When later, as Secretary of State, he came into contact with the representatives of other countries, he knew the background against which their careers were set and was acquainted with the public opinion of which, even then, they could never wholly lose sight. During the course of his travels, St John learnt French and Italian, and acquired a cosmopolitanism which was to stand him in good stead. The importance he attached to languages is further emphasised by the fact that he took the trouble to learn Spanish when he was already in office so that he might be no longer dependent upon possibly inaccurate translations of the documents it was necessary for him to read. Thus, during the negotiations which led to the Treaty of Utrecht, he was able to estimate the position which the circumstances of their respective countries would compel the statesmen of the different powers to adopt. He had the inestimable advantage of having studied foreign affairs in his youth on the spot.

St John was thus at considerable pains to acquaint himself with the language, customs, and political conditions of the countries he visited, and this fact is the more important in view of the prominence given by all writers to his immorality at this stage of his career. Goldsmith tells of an old man who had seen St John and some of his companions, in a state of inebriety, running naked across St James's Park. Another biographer assures his readers that St John 'avowedly made his relative, Rochester, his model; and endeavoured in every kind of debauchery to surpass his original'. The late Arthur Hassall writes of his 'riotous life' which 'alarmed his relations', though it is possible that they were not so easily shocked as Mr Hassall. Even Sir Winston Churchill wags a reproving finger when he describes St John as 'a roysterer and hard-drinker, who lived notoriously with a Miss Gumley'. Indeed, if the majority of the stories told about his excesses were to be believed, it would be impossible to discover how St John found time for any other occupation than that afforded by indulgence in wine and women. Such being the case, one is tempted to wonder whether, had he been on the winning instead of the losing side in the political struggle of his day, quite so much would have been handed down to posterity concerning his dissipation.

St John entered the House of Commons in 1701 for the borough of Wootton Bassett, and from the first he voted with the tories, who were then in a majority. Few men have made so considerable an impression upon the House of Commons at their first entry. He was, on the evidence of his contemporaries, an accomplished and persuasive speaker, who knew how to adapt his argument to the mood of his audience. Not a single speech exists which can be said to be anything like a correct account of what he said, but his written works are sufficient evidence of the vigour and style of his diction. His appearance, too, was eminently in his favour. Tall and graceful, he combined a commanding presence with a pleasing address. Above all, he had the advantage of entering parliament as a member of the opposition, for although his party was in a majority, it was opposed to the policy of William III and his ministers. Such were the position and circumstances of this young MP of twenty-two, who was to be a Secretary of State at thirty-two, and was to be deprived of office for ever before he was thirty-six.

His methods of attracting attention were well suited to the House of Commons as constituted in that parliament. 'You know', he wrote, 'the nature of that assembly; they grow, like hounds, fond of the man who shows them game.' As one of his biographers has put it: 'He had to show them game. He had by his halloo to incite the tories, to chase and worry whigs and dissenters, the directors of the Bank of England, and all who presumed to question the infallibility of the High Church party, and the supremacy of the country squires.' St John continued to adopt this policy when Anne came to the throne, and in November 1702 he was one of the sponsors of the Occasional Conformity Bill. In these circumstances there was general surprise when in the spring of 1704 he was appointed Secretary-at-War.

Various conjectures have been put forward as to the reasons for this appointment, and it has generally been surmised that St John owed his advancement either to Harley or to Marlborough. He was certainly at this time on the best of terms with Harley, and Marlborough may well have owed St John a good turn for his behaviour over the Act of Settlement. But it is surely not unreasonable to suppose that the new Secretary-at-War was chiefly beholden to Godolphin himself, the Lord High Treasurer. To that veteran parliamentarian the young member for Wootton Bassett had acquired a definite 'nuisance value', and the time had come to buy him off. St John was able, so he would not disgrace an office particularly important in time of war; and he was ambitious, so he was unlikely to look a gift-horse too closely in the mouth. Moreover, his appointment would bring some at least of the extreme tories to support a war for the conduct of which he was to be so largely responsible, while it would deprive those who still remained intransigent of their only capable leader. If Godolphin argued in this manner he made two serious miscalculations: St John was clever enough to retain his hold on the diehards, and he had the sense to resign when further complicity in a whig policy would have ruined his reputation.

If office did not reform St John, which was certainly not the case, he displayed a devotion to duty which surprised his contemporaries. He was the fortunate possessor of a constitution which allowed him to indulge in excesses without so impairing his health that he was unable to transact business. How long he would have been able to burn the candle at both ends in this way it is impossible to say, and his early fall from power may well have saved his life. If the Secretary-at-War worked hard, he did so by fits and starts. He would sit up all one night dealing with the work of his office, and the next he would spend with some friends over the bottle. Often he would be at his desk from ten in the morning until eight at night without taking any refreshment, but he never relapsed into carelessness. If he was sometimes unreasonable with his subordinates, he was equally so with himself. St John was never a good-natured man, but at this stage of his career he was, save by his political opponents, generally considered a good-humoured one.

He remained in office until the autumn of 1708 when, under pressure from Marlborough and Godolphin, the queen was obliged to accept a purely whig administration. St John thereupon resigned, and there can be no doubt but that he was perfectly right in taking such a course. He could not have remained in the government without becoming a whig, while by resigning he regained all his old popularity with the tories. Nor was this all: his tenure of office had been distinguished, and he retired with the reputation of a capable administrator.

This experience stood him in good stead two years later when the tories came into office. St John was appointed Secretary of State for the Northern Department in an administration of which the effective chief was Robert Harley. For nearly a century after the Revolution of 1689 there were two Secretaries of State, and their duties were divided by a geographical division of the globe into Northern and Southern Departments. The Northern Department was concerned with British relations with the northern powers of Europe, while the Southern Department had to deal with France, Spain, Portugal, Switzerland, the Italian States, and the Ottoman Empire, as well as Irish and Colonial business and the work later done by the Home Office.

The labours of the Southern Secretary were not so great as may appear, for Ireland had its own parliament and administration, and he was little more than a channel of communication between the Lord-Lieutenant and the Ministry. The Home Office work was slight, for most of the existing functions of that department have been created by modern statutes. Thus the Secretaries in the reign of Anne may be said to represent the Foreign Office cut in two, with some miscellaneous business assigned to that department of it which dealt with the southern powers of Europe. St John's fellow Secretary was the Earl of Dartmouth, a son of the nobleman who had been so loyal a friend to James II, but was himself a mere cipher in the Ministry. His masterful colleague assumed control of both departments, and Dartmouth in fact was little more than an Under-Secretary.

Whatever view may be taken of St John as a man, there can be no denying the brilliance of his handling of foreign policy. His conduct of affairs up to and including the Treaty of Utrecht has, for consummate ability, rarely been equalled and never surpassed in the course of English history, and it marks for all time his influence upon national policy. It was successful because it was based upon the realities of the European situation, and not upon theories of his own or upon the facts of ten years before. St John realised that there were two wars: one against France, which the Allies had won, and another against Spain, which they had lost, or were on the point of losing. He never forgot that the original object of the War of the Spanish Succession had been to prevent a French hegemony of Europe. This was the basis of a policy which he had both the vigour and the knowledge to put into effect. He was in close contact with opinion in his own party, and he knew Europe in a way impossible save to those who have studied it on the spot. If St John had shown the same courage and intuition in home affairs that he displayed in matters of foreign policy, he might well have gone down to history as one of the greatest of British statesmen.

The new administration was bent upon peace, but not upon peace at any price, and in all the diplomatic discussions which have taken place between the English and the French down the centuries it is doubtful if England has ever been more ably represented than by St John. The Marquis de Torcy, the French Foreign Secretary, was no mean antagonist, as became the nephew of Colbert. Zealous, precise and punctilious, he was the eternal type of French diplomatist, who is confident that the world has been created for the benefit of France and who is determined to see that there is no interference with the wishes of the Almighty. Nevertheless, he met his match in St John, for, as Professor Trevelyan so rightly said: 'It was Greek meet Greek, and blade cut blade.' Each statesman knew that the other's need for peace was as great as his own, but St John had the disadvantage that the whigs had committed England to a policy which was incapable of realisation, though to depart from it would be an act of treachery to the Allies. The aim of both negotiators was to arrive at a preliminary settlement, which should then be put before the other interested parties at a conference. To negotiate with an enemy behind the backs of one's allies is never very creditable, though it is often done, but St John had at least the excuse that previous attempts to make peace had been wrecked by the obstinacy of the Emperor and the Dutch. The truth is that by 1711 none of the Allies had clean hands, or anything approaching them, and those who have criticised St John for his attitude have overlooked extenuating circumstances.

In July of 1711 Matthew Prior was sent to Paris, and after three months' hard bargaining a settlement was reached on the main points at issue between Britain and France, and the way was clear for the Peace Conference to commence its labours. This body duly met at Utrecht on January 29, 1712, but before long it reached deadlock over the future of the Spanish Netherlands. When this difficulty arose St John adopted the time-honoured device of leaving the Conference to mark time while the real business was transacted elsewhere, in this case directly between London and Paris. 'Her Majesty is fully determined to let all negotiations sleep in Holland', he told the British representatives at Utrecht.

During the whole of the negotiations St John—or Bolingbroke as he had now become—was the principal factor on the British side, and on one occasion he went over to Paris, where he saw both Louis XIV and Torcy. Finally the Treaty of Utrecht was concluded. Bolingbroke allowed his sense of the dramatic full play. About two o'clock in the afternoon of Good Friday, April 3, 1713, a post-chaise rattled down Whitehall: as it stopped at the Cockpit there alighted, all covered with dust, Bolingbroke's half-brother, George St John, with the treaty in his hand. The Secretary welcomed him on the doorstep with open arms, exclaiming: 'It is the Lord's work, and it is marvellous in our eyes.'

The Utrecht settlement marks the apogee of Bolingbroke's career: he was still only thirty-four when he greeted his half-brother that Friday afternoon in Whitehall; but the summit had already been reached, and what lay ahead was in no way comparable with what had gone before. Nevertheless the conclusion of peace was in itself sufficient to put him in the front rank of his country's statesmen. There is much to be said against the methods he employed to effect a settlement, but in this matter any responsibility must be shared by his whig predecessors in office who had, for party reasons, rendered it impossible to conduct negotiations in any other manner. As for the Treaty itself: its great merit was that, like the Peace of Westphalia, it recognised existing facts. France was the first power on the mainland of Europe; Philip V was the monarch desired by Spain; Britain was building a colonial empire; and Prussia and Savoy were rising states. All these incontrovertible realities were admitted at Utrecht. At the same time precautions were taken to prevent the pre-eminence of France from developing into hegemony, just as the recognition of Philip was a check to any Habsburg inclinations in the same direction. It was all eminently reasonable, and in its main outlines it endured for more than two generations, which is as far ahead as any statesman can be expected to look.

Comparison of the Utrecht settlement with the treaties of Vienna and Versailles is inevitable, if somewhat profitless. In 1815 the negotiators endeavoured to make the world safe for autocracy, and in 1919 they attempted the same task on behalf of democracy: in both cases they proved to be giving mankind the exact opposite of what it desired. Bolingbroke and Torcy ignored such general principles; they dealt with the real, not with the ideal; and their work stood. Much can be said against Bolingbroke both in his public and private capacity, but it cannot be denied that he was a good European, and it was as such that he negotiated the Treaty of Utrecht. It was his greatest service to his country.

Had Bolingbroke been able to have his way, the Treaty of Utrecht would have been followed by a commercial agreement with France and a large step in the direction of freedom of trade between the two countries. In this respect, however, he was too far in advance of his age. The manufacturers rose in revolt, the whigs did everything in their power to foment the opposition, and a number of tories voted against the Ministry. Bolingbroke was no longer in the Commons to sway members by his eloquence, and more than one of his colleagues was only too ready to give him a fall. The vital clauses in the proposed treaty were rejected by nine votes, and a commercial understanding with France had to wait until the time of the Younger Pitt.

The story of the next few years does not redound to the credit of Bolingbroke. It is not easy to tell from his taking up Jacobitism what he really had in mind unless it was the restoration of James as a tory puppet. Being utterly without principle himself, it never seems to have occurred to Bolingbroke that the exiled Stuart might prefer his religion to a throne. When such proved to be the case Bolingbroke was without a policy. At the critical moment of the death of Anne he lost his nerve, and shortly afterwards he fled the country. For a space he was Secretary of State to James at the court-in-exile in France, but he was rightly dismissed under a cloud. Subsequently he obtained a restricted pardon from the British government which enabled him to reside in England when he felt so disposed. Had he died at this time he would be remembered today as the chief architect of the Treaty of Utrecht, but on no other score. However, once the use of power was out of his reach, he began to write about the theory of it, and in this way came to exercise a further influence upon English politics.

Disraeli declared that Bolingbroke was 'one of the ablest men who ever lived', and when he made this statement he was thinking in terms of home, rather than foreign policy, particularly of *The Idea of a Patriot King*, which was published in 1749. The book is an appeal to discard the party system and everything for which it stands. According to the author 'a limited monarchy is the best of governments', and a hereditary monarchy the best of monarchies. 'The good of the people is the ultimate and true end of governments', and 'the greatest good of a people is their liberty'. The best way to provide for the continuance of that liberty is by securing the accession of a Patriot King who, though eschewing rule by divine right, will equally refuse to be the mere figurehead of an oligarchical faction. He will be a constitutional monarch, whose power is limited by his consent to exercise that power subject to public opinion expressed in a free parliament. Under him corruption will cease, for a Patriot King has no reason to be corrupt. 'He is the most powerful of all reformers, for he is himself a sort of standing miracle so rarely seen, and so little understood, that the sure effects of his appearance will be admiration and love in every honest breast, confusion and terror to every guilty conscience, but submission and resignation in all.'

It is, of course, difficult to resist the conclusion that a great part of this famous treatise had no other purpose than to flatter the Prince of Wales, Frederick, who might one day be in a position to restore Bolingbroke, and also to belabour the whigs. Yet much of it is of permanent value, and has had its effect upon English history. The conception of the monarch as standing above the parties, representing the national interest as opposed to purely factional interests, was for many years to be the tory interpretation of the kingly office. Disraeli, in particular, always professed his agreement with the arguments advanced in *The Idea of a Patriot King*.

It was not Frederick, but his son George III, who attempted to put into practice the theories of Bolingbroke, and to no inconsiderable extent he succeeded. The decline of Jacobitism assisted him in a marked degree, since it regained for the ruling monarch the support of those who were naturally the bulwark of his throne, but who had been in opposition for two generations. Furthermore, the whig oligarchy was becoming divided and enfeebled, and, after the collapse of the Elibank Plot in 1753 had shown that the danger from the Jacobites was at an end, the whigs could no longer claim that they alone stood between England and the rekindling of the famous fires of Smithfield. George III too, even if devoid of the higher gifts of statesmanship, knew exactly what he wanted, and this is so rare a characteristic in English political circles as to give its possessor a natural advantage over his rivals. George intended to be a Patriot King of the Bolingbroke type, and by the exercise of the royal authority to ensure that the quarrels of the factions were subordinated to the interests of the nation.

How far he might have gone towards the achievement of this goal in ordinary circumstances it is impossible to say, but the American war and his own health proved his undoing. Yet George III never abandoned the attempt to enhance the power of the Crown, and so strong was it even after the loss of the American colonies that the king was able to have his way about Catholic Emancipation in 1801. Six years later he scored an even more notable triumph: he forced the 'Ministry of All the Talents' to resign although it had a majority in the House of Commons, summoning the Duke of Portland to form an administration. The result of the ensuing General Election showed that the king had interpreted the wishes of his subjects correctly. All this was very much in the spirit of Bolingbroke's philosophy, but George's relapse into insanity and the unstable character of his eldest son may be said to have brought the experiment to an end, though until Victoria came to the throne the personal opinions of the monarch played an important part in the working of the Constitution.

Of Bolingbroke's own career it only remains to add that his death in 1751 marked in very truth the end of an era. The last man to hold high office under a Stuart was now passed from the scene, and children were already born who were to witness the accession of Queen Victoria.

To what extent can Bolingbroke, at more than two hundred years' distance, be regarded as having justified the claim he put forward in his epitaph? That he was in the front rank where foreign affairs were concerned must surely be admitted without question. His handling of the negotiations which led up to the conclusion of the Treaty of Utrecht was masterly, and in the conduct of his country's relations with its neighbours he has been equalled only by Castlereagh and Canning, and perhaps by Sir Edward Grey and Sir Austen Chamberlain in our own time. But for Bolingbroke the diplomatic history of the eighteenth century might have been very different. As a political philosopher he was not in the front rank, but he influenced policy from the grave, which it is given to few statesmen to do. In the rôle of a party leader, too, he made his mark, and in some ways he might be said to have created a precedent in this connection.

So much for the credit side of Bolingbroke's account. There are important items on the other side. In the first place he seems to have been a physical coward, and he lost his head in an emergency, as was clearly shown during the crisis at Anne's death. He knew nothing of loyalty save to his own interests, as his wife, Harley and James III experienced in turn. He could never resist an intrigue, whether of a political or an amorous nature. All in all, he constitutes an outstanding example of a statesman in whose composition there is a great excess of genius over character. Yet, for better or for worse, Bolingbroke left a definite mark upon English history, and whether his career is to be admired or regretted, it cannot be ignored.

Man of Mercury

Life and Political Career

A foolish consistency is the hobgoblin of little minds, adored by little state-
men and philosophers and divines. With consistency, a great soul has simply
nothing to do ... Speak what you think to-day in words as hard as cannon
balls, and tomorrow speak what tomorrow thinks in hard words again,
though it contradicts everything you said to-day.

RALPH WALDO EMERSON

'THERE are some characters that seem formed by nature to take
delight in struggling with opposition, and whose most agreeable hours are passed in storms of their own creating.
[Bolingbroke] was perhaps the most indefatigable in raising
himself enemies, to shew his power in subduing them; and was not
less employed in improving his superior talents, than in finding objects
on which to exercise their activity. His life was spent in a continual
conflict of politics, and, as if that was too short for the combat, he has
left his memory as a subject of lasting contention.'[1] This was the view
expressed by Oliver Goldsmith in his introduction to Bolingbroke's
collected works.[2] It is a view which has not been radically altered since
their appearance in 1770, and all who have studied Henry St John, first
Viscount Bolingbroke, have been forced to recognise the vast inconsistencies in his character and in his writings. Even the biographers most
given to fulsome praise have seen that it is difficult to make an honest
evaluation of him, because, like quicksilver, he darts this way and that,
never resting but always active, never showing one face but always

17

many. It is impossible to form a complete and exact picture of any man, but some men are harder to bring into focus than others because of their fundamental elusiveness and will-o'-the-wisp character; Bolingbroke falls into this category. He is elusive not because there is any shortage of material: indeed quite the contrary, for there are not only his own writings but also many reports about him from contemporaries. Rather it is the man himself who presents the difficulty; such a controversial figure as he was, provoked conflicting reports both in his own day and ours. In writing about him therefore it is difficult to escape the Scylla of carping criticism or the Charybdis of unqestioning admiration.*

The eighteenth century was concerned about the judgments of posterity, and if Bolingbroke is indeed 'a superb figure at the gates of history',[3] then he should be judged by the accepted methods of posterity and history. The spirit of his age conformed to Hooker's opinion: 'The acts of every present age are most sincerely judged of by posterity. While men are living the judgment of their friends is perverted by love, the verdict of their enemies corrupt through envie.' Posterity, however, which tends to consider a man's merit rather than the man himself, and history which is, as Diderot thought it ought to be, the other world of the philosopher, has not been kind to Bolingbroke. Clever he is thought to have been, brilliant, witty, charming—a man whose gifts were to be envied but his use of them distrusted. A whig of the old-fashioned sort said he was very clever indeed but a damned silly ass. England distrusts cleverness, trusts only solidity. If Bolingbroke had been a Frenchman, his talents in the boudoir, the salon, the cabinet and parliament would have brought him greatness; as it is he is merely an Englishman to be discreetly forgotten—save by historical scholars who forget no one— or at best confused with the Bolingbroke of Shakesperian fame and royal destiny.

He had the noble ancestry which the biographical writers of an earlier age generally thought fitting and indeed necessary for a noble subject to have. Because a man's ancestry was thought in some way to have a direct influence upon him, with ancient prowess bringing the

---

* There is great need for a major biography of Bolingbroke of the scope and precision of J. H. Plumb's study of Walpole. The best studies are by George Cooke (1836–37) and Sir Charles Petrie (1937). Walter Sichel's work (1901) is too laudatory and uncritical to supersede Cooke's. Petrie's book gives us the man and sets him very neatly in the Jacobite tradition, but it does not claim to be definitive. (See Select Bibliography, pages 158–59.)

possibility of renown in the living character, genealogical records were searched with the utmost diligence in order to accoutre the subject with an heroic past. Such was the eighteenth century's conception of the laws of heredity, and if these have any validity Henry St John would be by his antecedence a curious mixture. He could claim descent from a St John who came with the Conqueror. This St John had progeny who married into the remnants of the Saxon nobility and who later allied themselves with the Beauchamps, thus connecting themselves with the Tudors. The family prospered, ennobling itself by collecting titles and estates during the succeeding reigns. Fortune favoured them in the reigns of James I and Charles I, and peerages were awarded to the several branches of the family. With the inconsistency of nature, however, that was to appear so strongly in Henry St John himself, many of those who had received the most from the Stuarts were their most determined opponents. The two family lines of royalist and parliamentarian were united in the marriage of Walter St John and Joanna St John, and their son was the father of Henry St John, Viscount Bolingbroke. Thus he had in him both Saxon and Norman, Roundhead and Cavalier, the hard sense of the one and the picturesque nobility of the other—diverse elements that might well symbolise the twin aspects of his character: pure reason and wild romanticism.

Henry St John was born in 1678 at Battersea in the home of his grandparents, where his paternal grandfather Walter St John held sway like a Roman paterfamilias. Walter St John's son, Henry, the father of Bolingbroke, counted for little in the household for he was a rake and a beau in the full Restoration sense but was little else. His only claim to fame came when, as a youth, he was convicted of murder but bought his pardon from King Charles II for £16,000. His life of pleasure never ceased or lessened, and when his son was high in political circles he continued 'a man of pleasure that walks the Mall, and frequents St James's Coffee-house, and the chocolate houses'.[4] Even so, 'Old Frumps', as his son called him, perhaps achieved some distinction in living until he was ninety, and receiving a title from King George I when his son was a proscribed traitor and under attainder. Not for him the triumphs of public eminence, but neither did he suffer the bitterness of exile.

The young Henry St John lived far away from the riotous world of his father in the pious household of his grandparents. Later he complained of the dour drabness of his youthful home: its depressing character accentuated in his mind by plaintive recollections of being forced to read the writings of Dr Manton which consisted of one hundred and nineteen sermons on the one hundred and nineteenth psalm.[5] This is no doubt an overstatement of the case since youthful persecutions and punishments will often loom large in remembrance, but certainly the household at Battersea was far from licentious, and the puritan traditions of one half of the ménage were well in the ascendant. St John went to Eton, where, according to the not always reliable Horace Walpole,[6] he was to begin his rivalry with Robert Walpole: a rivalry which, if started at such a point, must be one of the longest in duration between two eminent personalities. After Eton there is a tradition that he went on to Christ Church College, Oxford, though the college records have no information on this point. Later he did receive an honorary degree from Oxford and was then put on the books of Christ Church; so it is perhaps from this that the tradition has developed. It may well be that this association, even though only an honorary one, made him feel himself to be a scholar by adoption, and he certainly was a scholar spiritually if not in intellectual ability. His later writings show both a depth of reading and a real interest in learning.

A gentleman's education was not considered complete without foreign travel, and in 1697 St John left England to travel on the continent. The sojourn there enabled him to learn several languages— French, Italian and Spanish—and to acquire a thorough first-hand knowledge of Europe. He went first to Paris, then to Geneva, Turin, Milan and Leghorn, being abroad for some three years in all. In addition to his social and academic expertise he acquired expertise in other fields, in drinking and wenching being fully initiated into the rites of Bacchus and Venus. His wild behaviour, which was clearly copied from that of his cousin the Earl of Rochester, the prince of rakes, did not lessen on his return to England. The days of puritan sobriety were behind him; it was reported he had run with other drunken youths naked through St James's Park. He lived up to the tradition of his class by gaining fame as the protector of several of the more notorious whores; and never overcame his reputation as a man of loose morals.

Indeed, he never ceased to be a lecher; Dean Swift commented later, 'Lord Radnor and I were walking in the Mall this evening: and Mr Secretary [Bolingbroke] met us and took a turn or two, and then stole away, and we both believed it was to pick up some wench; and to-morrow he will be at the cabinet with the Queen; so goes the world'.[7] Once gained, his reputation as a debauchee was to be the greatest of obstacles in his relations with Queen Anne; his abilities were overshadowed by his notoriety and his character was called to account by a raucous chorus of Mrs Grundies. 'His soul was all virtue, his body was all vice. A Stoic in the library, he was an Epicurean at the supper table and in the boudoir.'[8]

A superficial mantle of domesticity was placed over his shoulders when in May 1701 he married Frances Winchcomb, who was worth £40,000. The marriage was not a success, and each was probably to blame, the wife complaining of the husband's constant infidelity and the husband complaining of the wife's vile temper.[9] At the same time he entered parliament as a member for Wootton Bassett and began that shining career which like that of Lucifer had such a swift and sudden downfall.

He entered parliament in 1701 with the wild halloo of the sportsman and from the start acted as the whipper-in to the tory huntsmen coursing after the whig foxes. This was how he later described those early days in the Commons: 'You know the nature of that assembly; they grow like hounds, fond of the man who shows them game.'[10] Game there certainly was, and in abundance. The initial victims were the ministers who were in office at the time of the signing of the partition treaties, negotiated by William III and Louis XIV, which divided the Spanish lands between the rival claims of Bourbon and Hapsburg. The fact that the treaties were realistic, preventing the hegemony of either Bourbon or Hapsburg, was irrelevant. The ministers involved were whigs, and the tories had taken to horse against them; it was purely partisan politics. The ministers were impeached in the Commons, but a deadlock between the Lords and the lower house over the prerogatives and powers of the two chambers prevented the impeachments from being brought to a successful conclusion. Years later St John was to declare that the whole policy at this time was wrong, and that he admitted 'with some shame' the absurdity of his party's conduct.[11]

With a consistency not usually characteristic of tory policy, the country party proceeded to demonstrate its loyalty to the protestant cause by supporting, indeed introducing, the bill which gave the throne to the House of Hanover. The tories were content for the new king to be a constitutional monarch; they could hope to be the majority in parliament; they could thus govern the country. St John played a prominent role during the debates on the bill for the protestant succession and it was enacted into law. Thirteen years later, the tories found that they had in supporting the Act of Settlement created a situation which was to limit their own freedom of action. In addition to this bill for the protestant succession St John supported the Abjuration Oath which required all office holders to abjure any allegiance to the Pretender and to support the Act of Settlement. This new act implied that the protestant sovereigns were not only lawful but also rightful; and consequently it was an extension of the fiction that had evolved after the Revolution of 1688. At that time *de facto* allegiance had sufficed: now *de jure* allegiance was required as well. It may be asked how St John could act in this way when a dozen years later he was to seem to be of a very different mind, but absolute consistency in politicians is not always a prime requisite; nor is it always sensible.

In March 1702 King William died—unregretted and unmourned by any except a few intimates, for he had never been a popular figure. He was succeeded by his sister-in-law Anne who was accepted by all of her subjects with enthusiasm. She was English, a Stuart, a staunch Anglican and a sovereign by the will of parliament; all of the necessary qualifications were combined in her person to satisfy all parties. In addition her accession postponed the inevitable day of the Hanoverian succession, for which few, even of those who supported it as a political necessity, felt any marked enthusiasm.

The election which followed her accession saw the tories once more in a majority in the Commons, but with the whigs still predominant in the Lords and a strong influence in the administration. The party game was now played in earnest, and St John with his boldness and dashing oratorical style led the 'high-flying' tories to the attack with an indictment against Lord Ranelagh, a former whig office-holder, who was charged with fraud and theft and was finally expelled from the Commons. With the scent of blood in their nostrils the tory hounds were now coursing wildly. St John introduced the Occasional Conformity Bill: an avowedly partisan measure which aimed at penalising any office holder who, having taken communion in the Anglican church to comply with the provisions of the Test Act, continued to worship in a dissenting chapel. St John's observance of his religious duties was of the most perfunctory nature, as Swift recognised: 'I was early with the Secretary [Bolingbroke] today, but he was gone to his devotions and to receive the sacrament; several rakes did the same; it was not for piety, but employments, according to Act of Parliament.'[12]

Although personally not opposed to toleration, he considered the bill to be necessary for the good of the party and for the nation, arguing that it was 'neither unreasonable nor unjust. The good of society may require that no person shall be deprived of the protection of the Government on account of his opinions in religious matters; but it does not follow from hence that men ought to be trusted in any degree with the preservation of the Establishment who must, to be consistent with their principles, endeavour the subversion of what is established'.[13] The tories showed here, as they had so often, that the preservation of the established church was the one thing they were prepared to defend to the death, even if the method of preservation was an unworthy one. The Lords, having a whig majority, rejected the bill though there was much pressure from the crown to accept it; even Prince George, Anne's husband, was prevailed upon to vote in its favour and did so while saying, however, to his whig friends, 'My heart is vid you'.[14]

The defeat of the bill in the Lords infuriated the tories still further and they cast about for new victims or new culprits, according to one's interpretation. Lord Halifax, the Nestor of the whigs, was selected as the object of their attack and he was accused of the misapplication of public funds. St John was appointed a commissioner to inspect his accounts and apparently discovered sufficient evidence to support the charges. But once again the Lords used the time-honoured method of controversy between the houses to prevent the impeachment of Halifax from being anything more than formal accusation. The whigs then decided that two could play the game of investigation and impeachment, and proceeded to institute some inquiries into the conduct of certain tories ostensibly associated with Jacobitism. This was very near the bone for many, but St John rescued his party by reversing the usual process of controversy and starting one in the Commons against the Lords. A paper war of resolutions and counter-resolutions followed; in the end no tories were investigated closely and the whig manoeuvre was a failure.

Another example of the temper of the times can be found in the Aylesbury Election case. Decisions on the seating of members and on electoral matters generally had been concluded in the past on a strict party vote; but in the particular case under consideration, which arose from the case of Ashby v. White, the matter under scrutiny was the right of an elector to cast his ballot. St John and others of his party in the Commons took the view that, as the house could decide disputed elections, so also could they decide on the right to vote. The Lords, however, took the view that the right to vote was 'original according as it was held from a freehold or burgage tenure in a county or prescription in a borough'.[15] Further, the Lords argued, it was for the law courts, not the Commons, to redress a grievance. St John contended that such a solution could not but lessen the rights and liberties of the people for he was convinced, at least at that time and on that issue, that royal influence and pressure could be exerted more on the judiciary than on the Commons. An impasse was therefore reached; placards like so many army standards were posted all over London; the unseemly imbroglio continued for several weeks until concluded by the queen's proroguing parliament.

In the midst of these skirmishes and diversions the government found it advisable to reconsider its policies and composition. As part of the process of the reconstitution of the ministry, St John was offered the post of Secretary-at-War which, to the surprise of many, he accepted. But how did this appointment arise? Any answer must of course be in part conjectural, but four rather diverse considerations governing his appointment may be suggested. The first is that he was so obstructive and so irritating that it would have seemed preferable to have him as an ally rather than as an opponent, and to have his talents at the disposal of the government rather than in opposition to it. Secondly, his appointment would please the more extreme tories, 'the October Club', whose spokesman he was, and would incline them perhaps to give their support to the ministry. Thirdly, he was a member of the Harley circle and as the ministry wanted Harley they had to take St John as well, for Harley would not take office without his young associate. Fourthly, there was the influence of Marlborough who had been excluded from Bolingbroke's attack on William's advisers and who was therefore under an obligation, and at the same time concerned to provide himself with a grateful protégé in an office where he needed support.

So in 1704 St John joined the government which ardently supported the war and which made possible the great victories of Marlborough. The Secretary-at-War received encomia from the duke who, in a letter to Godolphin, declared: 'I am glad that you are well pleased with Mr St John's diligence, and I am confident that he will never deceive you.'[16] The Secretary in his turn recognised Marlborough's prowess and renown; he was to write many years later that the duke was 'the greatest general' and 'the greatest minister' that England 'or perhaps any other has produced'.[17] St John was delighted by Blenheim and still more by Ramillies. He worked hard at his duties; indeed no one was ever to say that he was lazy—he enjoyed office, he was ambitious, and he obviously revelled in the sensation of power.

He kept his place for four years until 1708, but in the last two years he became increasingly dissatisfied with the policies of the government and even more with its composition. The whig element began again to dominate, Marlborough and Godolphin throwing more and more of their influence against the tories while Harley, the Secretary of State, became less and less of a power. St John decided that, although the immediate power of Marlborough was great, nevertheless Harley was a better ally; the more so since the latter had already begun to worm his way into Queen Anne's confidence through the influence of Mrs Masham. Besides, St John realised that he was definitely *persona non grata* with many of the whigs who would eject him from office at the first opportunity. So when the scandal of Harley's secretary's having passed confidential information to the French forced the Secretary of State out of office, St John went with him. He left office with the reputation of being competent and able; he had remained loyal to his friend and this loyalty had done him no harm at all. He recognised the astuteness of his decision when he declared to Harley 'that going out of employment at the time and manner we did was equally honest and prudent'.[18] Furthermore, he had shown to his friends in the tory party that he was not a whig and that he was loyal to the tory cause, or at least on the surface.

In the election of 1708 St John did not stand. There is no doubt that he could have been elected since Wootton Bassett was controlled by his family. However, his 'genius' must have told him that the events of the next two years would do nothing to enhance his career.[19] Consequently, instead of serving at Westminster he was to live in his country house at Bucklesbury. The town wits saw his retirement with sardonic eyes:

> From business and the noisy world retired,
> Nor vexed by love, nor by ambition fired,
> Gently I wait the call of Charon's boat,
> Still drinking like a fish, and ******* like a goat.[20]

Hardly complimentary, it was probably true, and therefore the more irritating. His reputation as a rake still haunted him, but few could believe that he wished the ghost exorcised in case he could no longer have the pleasures that gained him his notoriety. For the moment he was content to play the role of the country squire. He showed a keen interest in rural life, acted the part of a rustic philosopher demonstrating his powers as a man of learning, and in after years was to look upon this period as one of the most agreeable of his life. 'There has been something always ready to whisper in my ear, whilst I ran the course of pleasure and business, "*Solve senescentem mature sanus equum*". But my genius, unlike the demon of Socrates, whispered so softly, that very often I heard him not, in the hurry of those passions by which I was transported. Some calmer hours there were; in them I hearkened to him. Reflection had often its turn, and the love of study and the desire of knowledge have never abandoned me.'[21] These are sentimental reflections, perhaps only written for posterity, but certainly expressing his real feelings of the years 1708 to 1710. In his two years of rural existence he read much but often superficially. Yet his later use of his newly acquired knowledge clearly indicates that not all of his time was passed in carousing and whoring.

Although he was living in retirement his interest in politics did not diminish. He saw that his party needed new slogans, new vitality and new organisation. He had the good sense to see that the 'Tory party . . . had many votes but no tongue . . . a lingering prejudice haunted rural minds, and inclined them to prefer stupid magnates that shared it to clever ones who were emancipated from it. . . . [He] found the Tory party in a state of dumb power; . . . he became its spokesman and obtained its power.'[22] St John therefore discerned well the course he should take. 'There is no hope, I am fully convinced, but in the Church of England party.'[23] The whigs played into his hands by their impeachment of Dr Sacheverell, an unattractive cleric of strong tory prejudices, who during his sermons had compared the whigs, and particularly the unduly sensitive Godolphin, to Volpone. The proceedings taken against Sacheverell were farcical; the whigs 'had a sermon to condemn and a parson to roast', and they 'roasted him at so fierce a fire that they burned themselves'.[24] In the ensuing trial Sacheverell was found guilty but his sentence of suspension for three years was really an acquittal and the ministry perished in the flames it had ignited.

During the period of whig ascendancy Harley had indulged in the hazardous game of back-stairs intrigue, and the game had succeeded. By the summer of 1710 Queen Anne had released herself from the thraldom of the Duchess of Marlborough to whose influence she had long been submissive and had cast herself into the arms of Mrs Masham, Harley's creature. Dismissing her old advisers with a marked lack of ceremony and indeed consummate rudeness, she called in their opponents. Anne desired a ministry which was loyal to herself and not to a group elsewhere. Harley was chosen leader of this new government. He was not much inclined to a purge but did recognise that there were certain individuals, strongly partisan in activity if not in theory, on whom he would have to call. Henry St John was the most obvious of these, and Harley—apparently after some reluctance—offered him the post of Secretary of State. Thus began St John's rapid ascent to the top of the greasy pole of political power.

The general election of 1710, which returned a majority favourable to the tory ministers, saw St John once again a member of the Commons. The new ministry, while ostensibly representing a variety of interest, was actually 'the firm of Harley and St John'.[25] These two alone were the true policy makers, the others merely followed. Unfortunately Harley and St John could not sing for long in duet, and a feud was to develop for the solo role. For the moment, however, relations between St John and his colleagues could not have been more agreeable.

The new Secretary recognised why he and his associates had taken office. They had come 'to court in the same disposition as all parties have done; that the principal spring of our actions was to have the government of the State in our hands; that our principal views were the preservation of this power, great employments to ourselves, and great opportunities of rewarding those who had helped to raise us. . . . It is however true, that with these considerations of private and party interest there were others intermingled, which had for their object, the public good of the nation—at least what we took to be such.'[26] If these statements, written long after the events in question, really expressed the sentiments of St John and his colleagues, then their adoption of the principles of gross expediency, the Midas touch of political opportunism, may well explain the complete destruction that was later to befall them.

For the moment, however, the pressing question before the new ministry was the problem of the great war. Total victory and unconditional surrender were no longer the catch phrases of the leaders. St John and his friends sought to find a way to ensure the balance of power in Europe and bring with it political prizes and honour to all. St John was prepared to be the honest broker, but brokerage fees for such an operation were high, and clients would have to adjust themselves to meet his costs. Louis XIV was willing to consider negotiations on reasonable terms. However, before serious negotiations could be considered, English public opinion had to be moulded so that when the actual news of the government's plans was published there would be no popular outcry at the turn events had taken. With public opinion shaped aright, the ministry could discount the opposition of an infuriated faction of the whigs. Harley and his colleagues were convinced that a good peace could be made, and they sought to get the public to agree with them.

To educate the public is not easy, but it was as a propagandist that St John showed his talents at their best. He marshalled a group of agents skilled in special pleading and launched a campaign to present the reasonableness of the government's programme. These agents worked well, and the public seemed much more inclined to accept the idea of peace. While in the process of converting English public opinion, the ministry intended to show France that if it did not accept peace now the war would be fought with increased vigour and it would suffer infinitely more. To force France to be more amenable St John planned a diversionary action in North America; an attack on New France was to be made which, if successful, would enable England to hold the colony as a hostage and pawn for future negotiations. Further, the Emperor was chivvied and chided for his slackness in military operations and given to understand that any unwillingness to extend himself in what was really his own cause might conceivably lead to England's coming to a separate peace with France.

St John's preoccupation with foreign affairs did not lessen his awareness of domestic problems. The newly elected parliament needed considerable supervision and care. It was filled with youthful backbenchers of high tory persuasion who had formed the violently anti-whig and ultra-reactionary October Club. St John allowed this group to have its way over the Landed Property Qualification Bill: a bill designed to limit the political influence of the purely monied class by effectively confirming political power to the landowners. The theory behind the bill was that the landed rather than the commercial classes should represent the country, and that land was a more truly national source of money than the ephemeral activities of the business community. In reality it was plainly and simply a bill to keep down, as far as possible, the rising commercial classes; it was one of those desperate measures which are introduced by a class that sees its authority on the wane. Such sectional and partisan legislation as this, resembling the legislation of the *optimates* in their conflict with the *equites* in the last years of the Roman republic, demonstrated still further the attitude and outlook of the party to which St John had linked his abilities and ambitions.

He proceeded quietly but firmly in his negotiations for peace, sending his trusted agent Matthew Prior to represent him, but always keeping the general direction of affairs in his own hands. Whatever criticisms may be levelled at St John it cannot be doubted that he was one of the most able men ever to control a country's foreign policy.

Unfortunately it was precisely at this very crucial juncture that relations between Harley and St John began to deteriorate. The two men were too dissimilar in character to work harmoniously for long. 'Harley was the sort of man who would drift past opportunity on the tide; while Bolingbroke might be apt to run his boat upon the rocks without waiting for a landing place.'[27] Harley had grown increasingly jealous of the prestige and influence of his former protégé, while St John, for his part, had become excessively dissatisfied with his former patron's vacillation. Harley's prestige with the queen, the ministry and parliament had been declining considerably and it was only restored by the unsuccessful attempt of the Marquis de Guiscard to murder him. Popular sympathy veered round to the injured minister. St John himself, one suspects, would have shed only crocodile tears if his rival had been so timely and completely removed by death. Upon his recovery and restoration to the direction of affairs, Harley's position was further enhanced when he was created Earl of Oxford and made Lord High Treasurer. But his colleague noted: 'he [Harley] stands on slippery ground, and envy is always near the great to flip up their heels on the least trip they make'.[28] St John the adroit was ever ready and willing when the occasion warranted to seize his opportunity and to overthrow his erstwhile friend.

St John was now his party's acknowledged leader in the Commons, where his talents were displayed to their best advantage. He worked diligently at his office, organised his party, spoke with brilliance, and controlled the house; yet he was still the beau and the lecher: an Alcibiades combining business and pleasure. For his contemporaries

> [he had] an irresistible fascination . . . There was about him still the charm of youth combined with the authority which the administration of great affairs naturally confers. The two

studious years in his country retirement had given him a knowledge of books which he had not previously possessed; and he
seemed not only to be a man of business, but also a man of
learning . . . His pleasant wit and keen intelligence enabled him
to make the best display of all that he had. His statesmanlike
capacity could scarcely be denied by his bitterest enemies . . .
His manners were courteous without being studied . . . His
conversation was pleasing; in private society he was gay, natural
and frank; he spent his money freely . . . A good natured man,
perhaps he could not be justly called; but he had at least the
appearance of good humour; and even his vices seemed akin to
generosity rather than self-seeking ambition.[29]

But, as Plutarch said of Alcibiades: 'His greatest abilities in politics, his
eloquence, his . . . genius and keenness of apprehension were tarnished
by his luxurious living, his drinking and debauching . . . The great
men . . . saw his behaviour with uneasiness and indignation, and ever
dreaded the consequence.'

When the rumour that the ministry was negotiating with the
French finally reached the ears of the whigs they reacted like men
possessed. Debate in both houses grew heated. With St John skilfully
parrying all attacks in the Commons, the ministry there was in little
danger, but in the Lords, Harley, no longer as supple and adroit as he
once was, made an inadequate showing, and the government was
unable to secure a majority of peers to support its policy. Defeat in the
Lords would mean all was lost; the whigs openly exulted. St John,
however, was not lacking in resourcefulness. He and Harley, reunited
by the crisis, persuaded the queen to create twelve new peers in order
to swamp the opposition. The latter were indignant at what they considered an unjustifiable extension of the prerogative, and in their fury
vowed to be revenged on St John. But for the time being he had
triumphed. There were no further obstacles to peace.

In the summer of 1712 St John was elevated to the Lords as Viscount
Bolingbroke. He had refused a peerage when the great crisis had
occurred because it was evident that his talents were then needed in the
Commons. He took the peerage partly from a desire to glorify still
further the name of St John, and partly because he thought that he
could serve his party and himself better in the upper chamber. It was
an extremely foolish decision; his talents and powers were such that he
was more influential in the Commons than he could ever hope to be in

the Lords. One is tempted to compare his decision with a similar one made by Henry Brougham, whose career was severely impaired when he accepted a title. Indeed, Brougham and St John resemble each other in more than one respect, for each had a brief heyday of power and a long and sad twilight of isolation and frustration. Nor did St John's ennoblement satisfy his pride and ambition. He wanted an earldom: all Harley would offer was a viscountcy. This made him very bitter against Harley. He even tried to have the patent halted, but it was too late. With the appearance of Viscount Bolingbroke the schism between the two leaders was complete.

To speed the final decisions on the treaty, Bolingbroke participated directly in the negotiations and went to France to confer with the French representatives. So well did the negotiations progress that Ormonde, the commander of the army, was instructed not to engage in any hostile actions; in short, there was an unofficial armistice. Bolingbroke found the *ambiance* in Paris much to his satisfaction; the populace cheered him, the official world respected him, and he won the favours of the beautiful Claudine de Tencin. The time passed all too quickly; soon he was required to return to England and the sombre surroundings of the council chamber. He came home almost like a Roman hero, crowned with the laurel wreath and hopeful of a triumph. Unfortunately too much success breeds envy. Even the queen was slightly irritated with him for having received such a flattering reception in Paris. She and his associates combined to curb his power but this was not to last. It was evident that Bolingbroke's sure skill was essential for a satisfactory conclusion to the treaty. The successful conclusion of it in April 1713 restored his authority in full measure. Trevelyan says: 'Thanks to the party bond, the Tories under Oxford and Bolingbroke adhered together long enough in office to force through the difficult and indispensable peace of Utrecht.'[30]

Bolingbroke's prestige was at its zenith. Even so, he could not persuade his countrymen to accept the commercial treaty with France which he had promoted vigorously. Various factions gathered in the lairs of opposition and he was unable to smoke them out. Furthermore, his colleague Oxford did little to support the proposed treaty, being influenced in all probability not so much by actual dislike of the treaty as by irritation at Bolingbroke's successes. The commercial treaty was defeated by nine votes.

Though worsted on so important an issue, he still had his old magnetism and ability to charm the public. On the occasion of the first presentation of Addison's *Cato*—a play designed to provoke tory wrath—Bolingbroke took up the whig challenge. At the end of a long speech by the leading character lamenting the loss of liberty, Bolingbroke rose from his seat and congratulated Booth, the actor, for presenting such a notable oration against a dictator: a palpable hit against Marlborough. He heightened the effect of his ploy by bestowing on the actor a purse of fifty guineas. The theatre echoed with cheers, the town buzzed with the story, and even the whigs had to admit the success of his gesture.

All this, however, was but a prelude for the real-life drama that was about to occur. Queen Anne was obviously in poor health, not indeed in any immediate danger, but still far from her full vigour. What was to come after had now to be decided. By law the Elector of Hanover was to succeed, but was this the real desire of Bolingbroke and his circle? He had certainly communicated with the Pretender's court, as had almost every other statesman of the day at one time or another, and, albeit he had spoken and voted for the Act of Settlement, he had never indicated any great enthusiasm for the Hanoverians. Yet the claim that has been made that Bolingbroke was for the Jacobite cause cannot be proven. He was fully aware that, although support for the Pretender meant support for the legitimate monarchy and the restoration of the true royal line, the accession of a catholic prince was utterly out of the question, protestant sensibilities and suspicions being what they were. It would cause a defection from the tories and guarantee whig ascendancy.

Yet if James Edward's religion was the great obstacle, it could be argued it was the only serious obstacle. Let him conform to the Church of England, as his ancestor, Henry IV of France, had done to that of Rome, and his accession would become a practical political possibility, for the great majority of Englishmen would rally to the legitimist cause, if 'protestantised'. The Act of Settlement was the law of the land, but this could be repealed. Had not Mary and Elizabeth Tudor succeeded to the throne even though at one time they had been branded illegitimate and disinherited? Had not the Stuarts been barred from the throne by act of parliament and yet received the crown? And had not the entire Beaufort family at one time been expressly forbidden any rights of succession, and yet from this family came the Tudor claim to kingship? A mere statutory provision was not in itself sufficient to prevent the circumstances in which 'the King over the Water' could come into his own.

The real difficulty was that the tories were not at all certain about how they should proceed. The whigs, however, had no doubts; they were ardent Hanoverians, for they had nothing to gain from any other course. All that concerned the ministry was the short-term problem of how 'To break the body of the Whigs, to render their supports useless to them, to fill the employments of the Kingdom down to the meanest with Tories. We imagined that such measures, joined to the advantages of our numbers and property, would secure us against all attempts in her reign; and that we should become too considerable not to make our terms in all events which might happen afterwards; concerning which, to speak truly, I believe few or none of us had any very special settled resolution.'[31]

The ministry's policies were at best pragmatic, and at worst confused. The army under the Duke of Ormonde was officered wherever possible by loyal tories, and it was planned that strong party men should replace the waverers. But all of this would take time, and time was not available. Moreover, all the packing of the army and civil service was useless without a protestant prince from the Jacobite line, and this prince simply did not exist. Bolingbroke later declared:

> There was no design on foot during the last four years of Queen Anne's reign to set aside the succession of the House of Hanover, and to place the crown on the head of the Pretender to it . . . Neither could a design of that nature have been carried on so long, though it was not carried into execution, without leaving some traces, which would have appeared when such strict inquisitions were made. . . . But laying aside all arguments of the probable kind, I deny the fact absolutely; and I have the better title to expect credit, because it could not be true without my knowledge, or at least suspicion, of it: and because even they who believed in it—for all who asserted did not believe in it— had no proof to produce, nor have to this hour but vain surmises, nor any authority to rest upon but the clamour of party.[32]

There might have been just enough irresolution in the tory party to confirm Bolingbroke's statement. That is to say, the party was too undecided to have produced, even for consideration, a really thought-out plan for the restoration of James Edward. For he had so compromised himself by his refusal to change his religious affiliation that

Bolingbroke and his associates were extremely reluctant to undertake the work necessary for his accession. Probably the best that one can say is that Bolingbroke had no policy other than that of an honest broker who intended to do the best that he could for himself and for his friends. However, brokerage is rather like gambling: selling short is risky, and it requires men of some determination to play the market. Oxford's stomach was not strong enough for a speculator; he would not join the game, and so had to be got rid of. He was removed from power by the same method that he had used in gaining it, namely intrigue. He had gained his ascendancy through Mrs Masham; she deserted him for Bolingbroke who had courted her and flattered her, and on July 27, 1714, Oxford was dismissed. Now was the time for the 'true' men to take over. But Bolingbroke was not sure enough of the tories in whose name he acted; he needed a secure foundation for the power he wanted and so, almost simultaneously with Oxford's dismissal, he communicated with the leaders of the whigs, and invited them to dinner.

The evening must have been an odd one; Bolingbroke's genius for tergiversation was to be tested to the utmost. The talk which ensued all concluded with Stanhope's observation: 'Harry, you have only two ways of escaping the gallows. The first is to join the honest party of Whigs; the other to give yourself up entirely to the French King and seek his help for the Pretender. If you do not choose the first, we can only imagine that you have decided for the second.'[33] In retrospect this meeting seems most extraordinary even for the machiavellian Bolingbroke.

Bolingbroke could not really hope to get his way with the whigs. He was not prepared to plunge the country into civil war, yet he had no constructive plan; he was merely a partisan personality without a party platform. He had come to the end; he was beaten. But his efforts to keep power and office had not been without significance. As Lord Acton saw it:

> The author of the peace of Utrecht is memorable in history for the greater achievement of having elevated Toryism for the moment to the dignity of a political theory... A rational system could be created for it only by one who did not share its superstitions. Bolingbroke, a man free from very definite family traditions, of a philosophical turn of mind that impelled him to look for principles, and with a love of enterprise that could not be curbed by the heavy responsibilities of wealth, at the same

time a profligate and an unbeliever, was predestined to be the theorist of Toryism.[34]

He had his forty-eight hours of power before his house of cards began to tumble. His political pre-eminence and the life of the queen hung on the same slender thread, and the queen's illness was mortal. The council advised that Shrewsbury become Lord High Treasurer, which was done; the next day Anne died. Bolingbroke pithily summed up the events of that crucial week: 'The Earl of Oxford was removed on Tuesday, the Queen died on Sunday. What a world is this. And how does fortune banter us.'[35]

In his introduction to Bolingbroke's *Works*, Oliver Goldsmith saw the situation in 1714 very cogently. 'With as much ambition, as great abilities, and more acquired knowledge than Caesar, he wanted only his courage to be successful; but the schemes his head directed, his heart often refused to execute; and he lost the ability to perform, just when the great occasion called for all his efforts to engage.'[36] The play was now terminated; the proclamation of George I symbolised the dropping of the curtain; and all that remained was one long and melancholy epilogue. The events which were to follow did not form an epic decline and fall, but only a satirical rake's progress.

The new king had appointed regents to act in his name until he arrived; Bolingbroke's name was not on the list. He continued to hold office but he was only a figurehead. The whigs had won, and 'George the First was a party king as much as James the Third would have been'. Soon rumours were rife of a proscription in the Roman manner; Bolingbroke and Oxford were to be sacrificed on the altar of whig supremacy by opponents intoxicated with their new-found power. Terrified by this new threat he turned for help to Marlborough whom only lately he had treated with such contumely and cavalier disdain. The duke, relatively indifferent to party but most conscious of his honour, would not have been human, bearing in mind the recent actions of the all-powerful Bolingbroke, had he not taken a certain pleasure in this turn of events. The protégé who had become his patron was now his suppliant. Marlborough calmly informed Bolingbroke that Oxford had made a compact with the whigs, and that Bolingbroke rather than the former Lord High Treasurer would suffer the extreme penalty.

Without questioning Marlborough's motives or his sources, and knowing the extremity of partisan spirit then rampant, Bolingbroke at once took refuge in flight. He had refused to face his opponents courageously and to risk the block. By this he had shown the real weakness of his character and the superficiality of his philosophy. 'The fatal defect of his career is that he obtained power before he had learned self-discipline and when adversity taught him self-discipline he never obtained the necessary power. Had he, like Harley, defied his opponents in 1714 to do their worst he could in two or three years have emerged to be again a powerful figure, with no past to purge, and like Disraeli after 1846, lead a re-educated party back to a Promised Land. The clothes of the Whigs were there for the stealing and Bolingbroke was the most adroit and unscrupulous of thieves.'[37]

With his flight all of his enemies roared that the traitor had been found out indeed. The whigs had already moved a bill of impeachment, and upon his non-appearance declared him a convicted traitor by act of attainder. Had Bolingbroke faced the crisis and shown no apprehension, his opponents would, at the most, have uttered threats and maledictions. It is most improbable they would have menaced his life. As it was, he had shown fear, and his enemies pursued him with relentless ferocity. Bolingbroke was the object of universal derision and scorn. Like Alcibiades fleeing from Athens to Sparta, Bolingbroke made for France. Here, so recently the scene of his universal approbation, he was received with politeness but without marked enthusiasm. There was a vast difference between Bolingbroke the attainted traitor, and Henry, Viscount Bolingbroke, Secretary of State.

His first action in France was to promise Lord Stair, the British ambassador, that he would enter no engagements that would be prejudicial to King George; but at the same time he treated secretly with the Duke of Berwick from the Pretender's court. In July 1715 he joined the Pretender's entourage as Secretary of State. If Bolingbroke's flight could be explained as a momentary mental aberration, this certainly confirmed that delusion had become fixed in folly.[38] He later accounted for having taken such a desperate act—an act which he never ceased to regret—by saying: 'The Whigs impeached and attainted me. They went farther—at least, in my way of thinking, that step was more cruel than all of the others. By a partial representation of the facts, and pieces of facts, put together as it best suited their purpose, and published to the whole world, they did all that in them lay to expose me for a fool, and to brand me for a knave.'[39] The reason for human action is sometimes hard to understand, but certainly public scorn and humiliation combined with loss of honour and a reputation for competence may account for acts that are fundamentally unreasonable and out of character. Bolingbroke's whole previous career had been based on doing what seemed reasonable and expedient, but this was fatuous in the extreme, neither intelligent nor prudent.

The exiled Stuarts were surrounded by conflicting factions: Irish against English, Scotch against Irish, protestant against catholic, men against women—all busily gossiping, intriguing and hoping for 'the great day of Jubilee': a great day which was never to come for such people as these. They were like the petulant patricians surrounding Pompey, eagerly awaiting the spoils, preparing the proscription lists and losing the future in the present.

Bolingbroke was appalled by what he saw at St Germains: an irresolute prince surrounded by pandering sycophants. But he had joined them and would act to promote their cause. He had arrived too late to direct the proposed invasion and insurrection, but he was instructed to use his influence with France and to foster amiable relations with its government. In addition he was to use his literary skills to help convert public opinion in England where there was still a great sympathy for the Stuart cause. Acting upon his instructions, he drew up a sort of latter-day Declaration of Breda which, like the original, was designed to allay all fears and to convince the country that the true royal family was worth a fight. Unfortunately, James Edward, who had already shown that he possessed more than the usual amount of obstinacy characteristic of his family, insisted in making a number of changes in the document. The Secretary's phraseology, and hence his meaning, was drastically altered by the prince's catholic advisers and his female confederates; the result was the most tedious platitude and gross ambiguity which could convince no one but the most ardent Jacobite.

Because of the inadequacies of Ormonde, the incompetence of Mar, and the weakness of the Jacobites in general, the rebellion of 1715 failed miserably. James Edward, who had directed part of its operations personally, shared the blame for the disastrous course of the rebellion. On his return to France, searching for a scapegoat, he turned on Bolingbroke and dismissed him from his service. Bolingbroke had hardly deserved such treatment. It is true that he had been indiscreet; his penchant for a pretty face had led him to confide secrets to Claudine de Tencin and she, having no real loyalties, sold her knowledge, which reached Whitehall. The Pretender had learned of Bolingbroke's indiscretions through his own adoring circle who were not partial to the

Secretary or his mistress. But, although the Jacobite plans were probably foreknown, such foreknowledge was hardly enough to account for the ignominious collapse of 'The Fifteen'.

With Bolingbroke's unceremonious dismissal his career as a Jacobite was ended. Later he was to describe the Pretender's court in the most vitriolic language, but for the moment it was on him that the abuse was poured. It was only a very few who perceived the realities of the situation. Lord Stair the ambassador declared: 'Poor Harry is turned out from being Secretary of State, and the seals are given to Mar; and they use poor Harry most unmercifully, and call him knave and traitor, and God knows what. I believe all poor Harry's fault was that he could not play his part with a grave enough face: he could not help laughing now and then at such kings and queens.'[40] And the Duke of Berwick, a truly loyal Jacobite, said: 'I owe him the justice to say, that he left nothing undone of what he could do, to move heaven and earth to obtain supplies, but was always put off by the court of France; and though he saw through their pretexts and complained of them, yet there was no other power to which he could apply.'[41]

His departure was regretted by very few at St Germains. The Irish disliked him because he was English, the catholic zealots because he was sceptical and protestant; the queen dowager, Mary of Modena, disliked him because he was a libertine, the women of the court because he did not take them into his confidence, Mar and Ormonde because he had ability. Above all James Edward disliked him because he was a realist and the Jacobite cause subsisted on romanticism. Moreover, the Pretender could never tolerate honest frankness as against servile mendacity. In addition, as if the hostility of the Jacobite court in France were not enough, his departure from the Pretender's services promoted new calumnies against him among the unenlightened tories in England.

He was now as anti-Jacobite as the most ardent of the whigs who were stirring up the vilifications against him, but his anti-Jacobite stand was for the time being quite valueless to him. He decided quite astutely on a new course of action. He began negotiations with Lord Stair to learn if a pardon might be obtained. The ambassador was sympathetic; George I was known to be merciful; but nothing more than promises was obtained, and Bolingbroke had to be content with these. Now that he was a doubly proscribed traitor he retired from Paris to the country. Here he played the role of the scholar seeking consolation in philosophy, and from his studies came the pastiche *Reflections Upon Exile* (1717)—

an imitation of Seneca's *Epistle from Corsica*. This brief essay by Bolingbroke is of little value. It calls into question the whole idea of patriotism, equating it merely to the physical well-being of the individual at the moment. Explained by enlightened self-interest his view of patriotism was crass indeed, and was at best merely a mask to hide his own rather indifferent behaviour. Certainly 'no man was ever less inclined voluntarily to spend his time in this sublimely celestial star-gazing. He was a philosopher only because he could not help it.'[42]

In addition to his philosophical writings, he wrote (1717) a most fascinating *apologia pro vita sua*. This took the form of a long letter, probably never sent, to Sir William Windham—the acknowledged leader of the tories in England. This *apologia* was well written; it reveals much, too much perhaps, for it shows him without loyalty to country, friends or self, and exposes the superficiality of his policies and ideas. Perhaps, however, it was less damaging than it might have been; the letter was not published when it was written, although its general tenor was known to a wide circle. Certainly, even by expressing casually to his friends some of the things which would have best been discreetly forgotten, he gave ammunition to the whigs without gaining any advantage to himself. But, as with the gambler, there was a chance that the spin of the wheel could just possibly bring a change of fortune.

Although his estates had been lost by his attainder, he was not in absolute penury since his own relations had not cut him off completely. He was still able to be the gallant, the lover, the wit and the charmer. He established himself in a pleasant country house at La Source near Orleans where he was joined in his exile by the Marquise de Villette, a niece of Madame de Maintenon. The marquise was rich and beautiful and she became his mistress. After his wife died, Bolingbroke and the marquise were married; this marriage, the second for both, was infinitely more agreeable for each of them than the life with the original spouse had been. With his new wife Bolingbroke gained a fortune, and from the profits of wise investments the couple were able to make their residence even more delightful. La Source was a sort of pre-rousseau-esque ideal habitation, with all of the comforts of life, and here Bolingbroke played the natural philosopher. He wrote much; he designed a summer house, considered religion and entertained himself with fireworks. He even had his own private Socrates when Voltaire came to stay. The future sage of Ferney was audacious in his lavish praise of his host and hostess, scattered compliments like snow flakes and even promised to dedicate his *Henriade* to the Philosopher of La Source. But Voltaire, like his host, was a realist, and kept the dedication of the *Henriade* for some more eminent personage than Her Late Britannic Majesty's erstwhile Secretary of State.

Rustic life is agreeable enough for many men, but for Bolingbroke it was frustrating. He wanted activity, and detested vegetating far away from public affairs. Knowing that nothing but complete and abject submission would satisfy Walpole and his friends, he went cap in hand and once more appealed for pardon. This time he was successful, and in 1723 he was allowed to return to England. It was not a complete restoration—he was pardoned for treason but neither his property nor his seat in the House of Lords was restored to him—but it was a beginning, and what had already been granted could surely be extended and enlarged. He importuned the king, the *maîtresse en titre*, even Walpole, for further concessions but could advance no further. In his irritation and despair he returned to the continent. From his residence abroad he started anew, but this time with more wisdom. His wife, using the well-tried methods of Lady Masham, approached the Duchess of Kendal, the royal mistress, an exceptionally avaricious and grasping woman who had already been given £11,000 when Bolingbroke was pardoned in May 1723, and gained her support once more. The duchess, on whose favour Walpole depended to some degree, used her influence; and Walpole, who had once said of his opponent 'May his attainder never be reversed and his crimes never be forgotten',[43] was forced to give way. It was arranged that the attainder would be reversed, and in 1725 Henry St John, Viscount Bolingbroke and Baron St John, once again came legally to life.[44] Walpole restored him grudgingly, however, and with much ungraciousness, and gave Bolingbroke only private rights, denying him the privilege of sitting as a peer. The whig leader recognised that if Bolingbroke ever regained his place in the Lords there was a very strong possibility of his being called to public office because of his outstanding abilities. Walpole, therefore, took no chances and, while the tiger was allowed his freedom, his claws were clipped short. Even a number of tories who might have welcomed an avenging tiger were not sure that they wanted the tiger named Bolingbroke.

As a private gentleman he retired to a country seat at Dawley and started life as a rural magnate-cum-philosopher as in former days at Bucklesbury and La Source. Old friends such as Pope, Swift, Gay and even Voltaire came to stay. Voltaire made Dawley his headquarters during his two-year sojourn in England, and Bolingbroke played the role of cicerone and teacher, explaining the English customs and constitution with equal brilliance.

But Bolingbroke found, at Dawley as earlier at La Source, that the rural life was far from satisfactory, and when an opportunity came to assume a more active life he grasped it. This occurred with the revival of the opposition to Walpole. Bolingbroke undertook to make the opposition into a more cohesive and effective force. He saw his task in the following terms:

> They who affect to head an opposition, or to make any considerable figure in it, must be equal, at least to those whom they oppose; I do not say in parts only, but in application and industry, and the fruits of both, information and knowledge, and a certain constant preparedness for all events that may arise. Every administration is a system of conduct; opposition, therefore, should be a system of conduct likewise; an opposite, but not a dependent system.[45]

Bolingbroke therefore engaged himself in this congenial activity of harrying the whigs.[46] In 1727 George I died. Walpole's fall appeared certain and for a time it seemed that fortune was to relent its bantering of Bolingbroke. But his hopes that the new king would replace Walpole by his opponents were dashed when the new queen, Caroline of Anspach, shrewdly realising the value of Walpole to the Hanoverian house, induced her husband to confirm him in power. She became his most ardent supporter, and was more assiduous in commending him to the king than any mistress would have been. Walpole ruled then because of his royal patronage and because he had created a great party welded together by self-interest and place-seeking. Bolingbroke's principal attacks on Walpole were on these grounds and he levelled his artillery at the joint targets.

His charges were given publicity in the political journal, *The Craftsman*, which, founded in 1727, appeared weekly and gained a wide circulation and considerable influence. The essays which appeared in it were extremely well written, with contributions from Pulteney, Arbuthnot, Swift and Pope. With bitter cleverness they poured scorn, sarcasm and contempt on all place-holders. The message preached was that all good Englishmen should eschew party and embrace country. Bolingbroke himself, while directing the campaign against Walpole, produced a number of pieces such as the *Dissertation Upon Parties* (written 1726-34) which foreshadowed his more famous *Idea of a Patriot King* (1738), and *Remarks on the History of England* (1726-34). The last showed clearly the author's view that the benefits of history 'consist in deducing general maxims from particular facts, then in illustrating maxims by the application of historical passages',[47] and by this mode of argument all royal favourites from the middle ages to his own time could be shown to be variant forms of Walpole.

The opposition created by Bolingbroke had a limited success when it compelled Walpole to abandon his excise scheme in 1733, but generally speaking at best the whigs were annoyed by rather than fearful of the opposition. The party in power continued to hold office, and even Bolingbroke's own allies began to tire of the role created for them by their champion. So despondent did Bolingbroke himself become with his lack of success that in 1735 he retired anew to France; this time, however, it was exile with a difference, being self-imposed.

Bolingbroke remained abroad for eight years, and this was the period of his greatest literary productivity. A number of philosophical essays were written on a variety of subjects.* His dissatisfaction with rural life, so patent in his earlier years, was now less apparent, for with advancing age he had come to accept the inevitable. Walpole was immovable and never again would the 'true and loyal men' hold office. Even with Walpole's final retirement in 1742 the long hoped-for coalition of patriots did not assume power; the whig coterie with another at their head continued in office.

'Old Frumps', Bolingbroke's father, died in his ninetieth year in 1742 and his son came at last into the family properties at Battersea. Here, where he had passed his childhood, he was to pass his remaining years. Increasing isolation, irascibility and melancholy were to be his constant companions, and with them came an added pessimism. The optimism of his youth had departed completely, as can be seen in his last and unfinished work, *Some Reflections on the Present State of the Nation* (1742?). Further signs of his impatience with the world may be found in the violent attack which he made on his old friend Pope whose *Essay on Man* had been dedicated to him and was written in part with philosophic notes from Bolingbroke's pen. Pope had circulated copies of the *Idea of a Patriot King* in an amended form. Learning of this, Bolingbroke—although Pope was now dead—proceeded to vilify his

* E.g. *Fragments of Essays* (1735-47?), *Idea of a Patriot King* (revised 1745-47).

old comrade. This attack on a devoted ally raised a fresh clamour of disparagement against him. It seemed that the complaints of the whigs had been justified by events: Bolingbroke was incapable of true friendship or true loyalty to anyone or anything.

In March 1750 Lady Bolingbroke died. Her estates, most of which were in France, were illegally attached by her relations; recourse to law was the only method of halting them, but the case, though ultimately going in Bolingbroke's favour, was not decided until after his death. He lingered a lonely widower, tortured by gout, rheumatism and finally cancer. Towards the end of his life, his friend and admirer Lord Chesterfield called to see him. He found the dying man calm in mind declaring that 'God who placed me here, will do what He pleases with me hereafter; and He knows best what to do. May He bless you!' Bolingbroke was inconsistent to the end; any reputation he had was only made to be broken and dissolved in his death for even his scepticism was finally abandoned. He died on December 12, 1751, and was buried next to his wife in Battersea church. Later two busts with suitable inscriptions composed earlier by Bolingbroke himself were set up to commemorate the pair.

With all of his many talents, charms, and abilities he was doomed to have only a limited success in all that he did. His writings have been deemed superficial. 'Philosophy and theology owe him nothing. He simply presents rationalism in its crudest form as it has filtered into his mind from without.'[48] As for his party, he cast that into outer darkness for half a century. 'From 1714 to 1760 it may be said to be sleeping. "It is not dead but sleepeth", dreaming in old manor houses and colleges and cathedral cloisters, of Charles the Martyr and the days of the Merry Monarch "when loyalty no harm meant". . . .'[49] His writings were shallow and his political life had been a flamboyant farrago, the inevitable result of his specious expediency. 'Three years of eager unwise power, thirty-five of sickly longing and impotent regret—or something like it—will ever be in this cold modern world the fate of an Alcibiades.'[50]

On History

To give an accurate description of what has never occurred is not merely
the proper occupation of the historian but the inalienable privilege of any
man of parts and culture.

OSCAR WILDE

THE unbiased factual approach to historical presentation is a
relatively new one; earlier historians were often as much
philosophers as chroniclers. In earlier days historians seemed
to be required to make their writing a conscious manifestation
of their philosophy. Every man might be, as Carl Becker has said, 'his
own historian'.[1] The selecting of facts and the writing of the events
exemplified a personal belief in some canon of truth. History was not
merely a pattern superimposed by personal prejudice upon external
events; there was an historical process which had a specific purpose,
and this purpose was directly ascertainable and precise. Without the
proper apprehension of this purpose, history as such did not exist but
was merely a chronicle without guidance and direction.

The eighteenth-century *philosophe* believed that history had an
immediate and specific value. Those who wrote history were at one
with their classical forbears in believing that history was philosophy
teaching by examples. There was a use for history: it provided examples
and portents for actions both now and in the future. History was the
basis for ethical actions, a handbook for statesmen; and history was the
judge because it was the mirror of providence.*

* Cf. Thucydides, *The Peloponnesian War*: 'The accurate knowledge of what

The clearest, or perhaps it is better to say least diffuse, explanation by Bolingbroke of his 'philosophy of history' is to be found in his *Letters on the Study and Use of History*. The first five letters expound his views on historians and on history, its purposes and its values. Under the influence of the classical authors (Herodotus, Thucydides and Polybius in particular), he was convinced that the historian should not only provide a meaningful narrative but should also be prepared to give a systematic account of his notions of history. For him history was more than the sum of its constituent facts: it was a set of well-illustrated philosophical principles providing an education for life and a basis for action. In all of Bolingbroke's many writings—both in the purely polemical as well as in those written from a more objective viewpoint —he attempts to use history, or rather the lessons of history, to deduce general 'maxims from particular facts' and then to elucidate the 'maxims by the applications of historical passages'.[2] Thus his personal philosophy of history was brought into a direct confrontation with actuality as he recognised it. Not that this is a very original approach since most of his generation did likewise, but his approach is perhaps more overtly didactic, more swayed by personal bias. It must be recognised that his motivations were generally lower than those of his contemporaries. While the latter attacked institutions, he attacked individuals; while they tended to tolerance, he sought revenge. His perspective of history was distorted by the narrowness of his political aims: his desire to revenge himself on his hated enemy, Robert Walpole, and the whig party which he led. In Bolingbroke's view there were a number of agencies for the consummation of this desire, and history happened to be the one nearest at hand.

Furthermore, it must be remembered that Bolingbroke saw himself as the classic example of the man of action: the man postulated in the writings of Polybius as the one best fitted for the writing of history.* He was convinced that his history would have an enduring value because he himself had been a maker of history, and as a result was unusually qualified to interpret the past. Perhaps he saw himself as a latter-day Thucydides: a great captain rejected by an ignorant society,

---

has happened will be useful, because according to human probability similar things will happen again.'

* It was Polybius' view that 'History will never be properly written until ... men of action undertake to write it'; and 'practical experience is of the first importance for historical composition'.

but nevertheless possessing the true vision which they could not have because they were bedazzled by the machinations of evil men.

As an accomplished orator and student of the art of rhetoric, he was well aware that an effective presentation of the argument is more than half the way to success in convincing the listener. He realised that the easiest method of scoring points was to destroy the adversaries' propositions in the first instance, and then to conjure up from the shambles that remained a more attractive structure. By this method of putting down self-created men of straw, his own arguments gained in plausibility as those of his opponents paled into insignificance.

In reasoned debate the least striking point is made initially, and gradually in a logical order the more significant material is presented. Bolingbroke begins his *Letters on the Study and Use of History* in this fashion. After a few preliminary and polite asides, rather like an orchestra tuning up before starting the overture, he jumps into the fray and, with that dashing style for which he was famous in the Commons, launches a slashing attack and impassioned denunciation of those who see in history only a pleasant and amusing entertainment. In this he is opposing those authors who offer a *chronique scandaleuse* designed only to titillate and to have no worthy aim. Those who seek to use history for such a base purpose are to be despised, and their opinions—if they have any, or if they could have any—are to be rejected as mere trivialities. Equally objectionable, he considers, are those who go to history merely to seek material for 'talk, to shine in conversation and to impose in company; who having few ideas to vend of their own growth, store their minds with crude unruminated facts and sentences; and hope to supply, by bare memory, the want of imagination and judgment'[3]—history is not a listing of kings and queens in orders categorical. Knowledge of such trifles might perhaps be useful at parties, particularly in the provinces where superficial knowledge may pass for wisdom, and the man capable of pouring forth unrelated information may seem to be a genius. But it has no more real value than the knowledge of whether Adam had a navel. Such students of history—and Bolingbroke would deny they were students—are too superficial to be worth more than the slightest notice; certainly too inconsequential to be the subject of lengthy debate, and too trivial to warrant any serious consideration. Whatever defence they could put up would be so weak that one blast of the wind of reason would serve to knock down their fortifications.

At the other end of the academic spectrum, he discerns the professional scholars who pass many hours in explicating texts, in investigating and collating manuscripts, in discerning minute differences in various editions and identifying obscure references; these it is quite absurd to regard as historians. They are at best skilled technicians, not scholars; they are the dredgers in the kingdom of scholarship. What, then, of those who see in history and historical writing only pure scholarship? Polybius, to whom Bolingbroke was deeply indebted, declared of such men: 'They spend all of their time in libraries and acquire generally all of the learning which can be got from books, and then persuade themselves they are adequately equipped for their task [i.e. scholarship and interpretation] . . . To inspect ancient records indeed . . . is useful . . . But to persuade one's self that such ability in research is sufficient . . . is quite foolish.'

One is tempted to concur with Polybius and Bolingbroke if one has the occasion to read even the titles of the monographs presented each year by advanced research students at the universities, for the subjects considered seem to be the negation of learning and only the highest form of pedantic diligence. Such men as support this approach to history are not content to cultivate their own gardens—their gardens of antiquarianism which might reveal the origin of life and the roots of human institutions. Instead they seek out a fact and having caught it, cling to it like leeches. Indeed, with this one fact, and because they have the interpreter's skill, they have expounded it as Bolingbroke says 'into every form that can be given . . . [and] they have supposed, they have guessed, they have joined disjointed passages of different authors, and broken traditions of uncertain originals, of various people, and of centuries remote from one another . . . they . . . leave no liberty untaken . . . to prop up a system'.[4] From no reality they envisage a whole world. Each from the same isolated fact constructs his own fantasy, despite disagreement with the fantasy of some other person, and—despite all of the tortuous manoeuvrings of the learned mind—the whole business, when properly investigated, may have no basis in fact at all. Yet such pedants, as Bolingbroke considers them, are nevertheless much esteemed and to them 'the whole tribe of scholars bow with reverence'.[5] Their contributions, however, to men and society are negligible.

Also there are learned savants who, according to Bolingbroke, are often dangerous perverters of the truth because they enter into their task with preconceived philosophies to which they bend and warp the facts. Having already a considerable knowledge of history, they seek to impose upon it a special pattern to which they subscribe, instead of allowing further evidence to modify their conclusions. Bolingbroke would agree that all scholars have some bias; but, although there is such a thing as honest bias, many of these learned men have rejected this in favour of an utterly dishonest bias. On the other hand, the existence of fashionable theories and prevalent philosophies tends to make history subjective, and if history speaks to our passions, as Bolingbroke would have us believe, then one cannot have an objective stimulus or at least one cannot really have a rational stimulus. While systems of history, ideally, may be rational, in fact they are only too liable to be subjectively teleological. To take Bolingbroke's stand that all historians are dishonest is to impugn the motives of too many notable men, not excluding Bolingbroke himself.

If all these students of history, then, are in intellectual cul-de-sacs from which there are no exits for them, why should men be concerned with the past? Is this concern merely a form of filiopietistic shintoism? Bolingbroke's view concurs with the idea of most of his classical predecessors: 'History is philosophy teaching by examples; ... We need but to cast our eyes on the world, and we shall see the daily force of example.'[6] It agrees also with that of a twentieth-century historian, Collingwood: '[History] teaches us what man has done, and then what man is.'[7] Bolingbroke, Machiavelli and Thucydides all agree that history is the handbook for statesmen, and that politics and statesmanship are the highest embodiment of social virtue.

In addition to this, however, there is of necessity a desire to explain how this valuable possession can directly serve man. Does mere knowledge of history and a recognition that it is a purveyor of warnings and portents suffice? If this were true, history would seem to be merely another version of the activities of learned factmongers whom he holds in such low esteem. But it is not necessarily so. 'A bare statement of an occurrence', Collingwood argues, 'is interesting indeed but not instructive; but when this is supplemented by a statement of cause, the study of history becomes fruitful. For it is by applying analogies to our own circumstances that we get the means and basis for calculating the future; and from learning from the past when to act with caution, and when with greater boldness in the present.'[8] Here history acts its true role. It presents experience, and experience is vital because, as Quintillian summed it up, *Nam in omnibus fere minus valent praecepta quam experimenta.* (An ounce of practice is worth a pound of precept.) Without experience man is a pedant—incapable, meddling and presuming. If a man be only this he cannot ask the right questions nor can he comprehend what is immediately occurring; in actuality, though physically present, he is really absent. The knowledge and experience which a study of history can provide must have the further additive of interpretive genius; yet genius alone will not suffice since it is only a form of imagination. Experience and genius combine to make the artist; experience alone tells why a thing is so, whereas the artist not only comprehends the fact that it is but also the why and the wherefore.

By using history, as history should be used, the first principles of philosophy can be obtained with the concomitant result that:

> Self love but serves the virtuous mind to wake;
> As the small pebble stirs the peaceful lake.
> The centre mov'd, a circle straight succeeds;
> Another still, and still another spreads:
> Friend, parent, neighbour, first it will embrace,
> His country next, and next all human race.[9]

A man with both genius and experience may shine with lustre, but if he only has his own experience and not that given him by the past his influence will be incomplete. He will be a sort of comet: 'a blazing meteor, irregular in his course, and dangerous in his approach; of no use to any system, and unable to destroy any'.[10]

But may we gain experience without actually participating in events? Experience may be actual—that is, our own—or vicarious—that is, derived from some other person or event. Both actual and vicarious experience can contribute directly to our development, and so when a man educated by history comes to take his place in the world he has a sort of treasury of experiential gold upon which to draw. Consequently he is not unprepared to make decisions, and if he has learned his lesson well in his youth he will be the more readily able to participate in large affairs. And, as it is well known that the gods are more generous with their favours to the young and that this favour is often withdrawn with advancing age, those who would make their mark would be well advised to spend time in studying history.

The knowledge of history does more than provide the vicarious experience of observing great and good men in action. Experience 'is conversant about the present, and the present enables us to guess at the future; so history is conversant about the past, and by knowing the things that have been we become better able to judge of the things that are'.[11] History also extends or broadens one's cognition of the world as a whole and of the individual's relation to it; and although in the ordinary course of events man does not attempt to comprehend all things or to encompass all time, some part of time is useful as a set of markers for a course of action. We are given a *Zeitweltanschauung*. 'Place is enlarged, and time prolonged in this manner; so that the man who applies himself early to the study of history, may acquire in a few years . . . not only a more extended knowledge of mankind, but the experience of more centuries than any of the patriarchs saw.'[12] This means that man has a more extended memory, and this extended memory he may bring into his consciousness for present use and to help him approach present situations with more than what Bolingbroke calls 'genius'.

There is, indeed, a conscious lessening of parochialism and a concomitant extension of urbane sophistication. Prejudices and narrowminded intolerances vanish, and this enlargement of the spirit enables man to use his faculties and his experiences in a vaster area. Nevertheless, one should not fail to see, amid the blurred lines of a distant landscape, the greatness of the national destiny of which one is part and which is magnified by history.

> The citizens of Rome placed the images of their ancestors in the vestibules of their houses; so that, whenever they went in or out, these venerable bustoes met their eyes, and recalled the glorious actions of the dead, to fire the living, to excite them to imitate and even to emulate their great forefathers. The success answered the design. The virtue of one generation was transfused, by the magic of example, into several: and a spirit of heroism was maintained through many ages of that commonwealth.[13]

Virtue is political virtue, and it is to be found both in widening one's comprehension and in celebrating piously the national past. History overcomes what seems to be distinct contradictions; on one level it speaks to reason by the interpretation of experience, and on the other it speaks to passion by its poetic presentation. It might be noted here that, in spite of all of the appeals to reason and to man's rational nature, it is recognised by Bolingbroke that history has all of the elements of poetry as well. While philosophy starts—if it be right philosophy—in reason, and may end with imagination, history starts with an appeal to imagination and then provides its conclusions with reason.

The unchanging yardstick of all historical studies, no matter how the study may be organised, is that of time; time, as a measurement of the moving process of events, makes it possible to isolate and contain the whole of an action. 'The beginning, the progression, and the end appear, not of particular reigns, much less of particular enterprises, or systems of policy alone, but of governments, of nations, of empires, and of all the various systems that have succeeded one another in the course of their duration.'[14] This contemplation *sub specie aeternitatis* is dissociated from the passions and sensations of the moment; the examples which are designed to instruct are seen 'through a medium less partial than that of [current] experience'.[15] Expedient revisionism is cast down; it may triumph temporarily but in the last analysis it cannot stand in the court of time. The Last Judgment is the eschatological function of history. True revisionism comes only with time.

> The villain who has imposed on mankind by his power or cunning, and whom experience could not unmask for a time, is unmasked at length: and the honest man, who has been mis-understood or defamed, is justified before his story ends. Or if this does not happen, if the villain dies with his mask on, in the midst of applause and honour, and wealth, and power, and if the honest man dies under the same load of calumny and disgrace under which he lived, driven perhaps into exile, and exposed to want; yet we see historical justice executed, the name of one branded with infamy, and that of the other celebrated with panegyric to succeeding ages.[16]

Here is seen in the greatest clarity exactly what history would do: namely, that it would be a great and timeless tribunal meting out justice; it was in fact substituted for God, acting as a judge of all men. The eighteenth century had substituted an abstract divinity of its own, which was, none the less, a different aspect of the same deity. As Bolingbroke puts it:

> The principal duty of history is to erect a tribunal, . . . where men and princes themselves were tried, and condemned or acquitted, after their deaths; where those who had not been punished for their crimes, and those who had not been honoured

for their virtues, received a just retribution. The sentence is pronounced in one case, as it was in the other, too late to correct or recompense; but it is pronounced in time to render these examples of general instruction to mankind.[17]

Is it possible to represent from a purely earthly viewpoint the christian idea of justice more concisely? While the rewards here represented *pour encourager les autres* are scarcely those of eternal damnation or eternal life, the rewards are there none the less. History is an addition to the kingdom of God and the latter-day of something that happens here and now. It is the practical application of the experience of time, and hence the great unifying force of time is enthroned on high. Time is the 'moving image of eternity', and time is the other name for history.

With this *Zeitweltanschauung*, man is placed amid the great progression of all events in which human beings have ever been involved, and a proper knowledge of time prevents us from imagining that the events observed in one's own life can be the consequence of spontaneous generation. This does not imply that they are not unique but that they have an organic relationship with the past, with the present and with the future. Events do not come singly; neither do they come as accident nor as chance. Man is not as isolated as he would often believe in his darkest moments, nor do the forces which seem to propel him have no direction. A proper study of history orients man and helps him to place himself inside time; no man can act outside of time.

But there is a very specific use for the divisions of time in history. Time on a basis of *post hoc ergo propter hoc* permits man to recognise that: 'Modern history shows the causes, when experience presents the effects alone: and ancient history enables us to guess at the effects, when experience presents the causes alone.'[18] This means that by knowing the past we may be ready for what might occur in the future. By recalling past events it is possible, as Carl Becker says, 'to anticipate (note I do not say "predict") the future'.

> Thus from the specious present, which always includes more or less of the past, the future refuses to be excluded; and the more of the past we drag into the specious present, the more a hypothetical, patterned future crowds into it also. If our memories of past events are short and barren, our anticipations of future events will be short and barren; if our memories are rich and diversified, our anticipations of what is to come are likely to be more or less so, too.[19]

This may open a number of avenues which could lead to some fairly doubtful conclusions. This need not be so if the word 'anticipate' is given its due emphasis; but anticipation may be corrupted to prognostication and this is hazardous in the extreme. To use the past as an absolute determinant for the future is to misuse history; indeed, should it be attempted, and some have done so, the chance of success is small. It is the same as the argument from analogy which 'is of the same inconclusive character as Induction by Simple Enumeration; and like it, rests on the general belief in universal connexions, and takes a conjunction of attributes as evidence of their connexion'.[20]

The genius of history, therefore, has some of the qualities of the Delphic oracle; its messages are couched in veiled language, and only those with extreme perspicacity know how to read them. Bolingbroke, however, would indubitably subscribe to the view of Thucydides that 'the accurate knowledge of what has happened will be useful, because according to human probability similar things will happen again'. It should be noted again that the emphasis is on 'similar' not identical. For Bolingbroke is cautious enough to define his position: 'We must rise from the particular to general knowledge ... Particular examples may be of use sometimes in particular cases; but the application of them is dangerous. It must be done with the utmost circumspection, or it will be seldom done with success.'[21] It is perilous 'to govern ourselves by particular examples; since to have the same success, we must have the same prudence, and the same fortune; ... since the example must not only answer the case before us in general, but in every minute circumstance'.[22] This is palpably impossible; for, while the old cliché that there is nothing new under the sun may hold true, it is equally true to say that history never repeats itself. Events may have a similarity, there may be fantastic coincidences, but things are not identical. There is always some minute deviation which, through the servo-mechanism of events, can alter the pattern beyond all outward recognition. How then can one apply the past? Bolingbroke uses the metaphor of the translator who does not give a literal translation but rather catches the spirit; so are we to catch the spirit of history, to divine the *Zeitgeist* and to 'conform ourselves to the reason' of history.[23]

The 'reason of history' is composed of a set of general principles by which man lives *secundum naturam*, and from it may be deduced a 'general system of ethics and politics'[24] which is in turn in accordance with universal experience. To conform oneself, therefore, to the 'reason of history' means in the first instance to turn to the facts of experience and their inspired interpretation which, as we saw earlier, was the role of history.

> By contemplating the vast variety of particular characters and events; by examining the strange combination of causes, different, remote, and seemingly opposite, that often concur in producing one effect; and the surprising fertility of one single and uniform cause in the producing of a multitude of effects . . . a man of parts . . . may sharpen the penetration, fix the attention of his mind, and strengthen his judgment; he may acquire the facility and habit of discerning quicker, and looking farther; and of exerting that flexibility, and steadiness, which are necessary to be joined in the conduct of all affairs that depend on the concurrence or opposition of other men.[25]

This implies that the new-found philosophy latent in the external facts of history will provide men with the basis for action in all spheres of ethics, politics and morality.

This is, in fact, putting forward the view that man's character is alterable by education alone or by environmental factors which supply him with the necessary example; as Jeremy Bentham would put it: 'I thought man needed only to be shown in order to do good.' And indeed Bolingbroke with Locke and a great number of his contemporaries held to the view that a man's mind at birth was a *tabula rasa* on which external experience made its impress and hence created the character. It is true that Bolingbroke also held the notion that a man's character was to some degree controlled by his natural constitution (that is to say, the old concept of humours). But, nevertheless, even with this view he thought that alterations could be made and actions so directed by proper experience that man, who had within him at all times the innate ability to be good, would be good. To him evil character is a result of 'excess, abuse, and misapplication of appetites, desires and passions, natural and innocent, nay useful and necessary', while good is the consequence of 'moderation and government, in the use and application of these appetites, desires, and passions according to the rule of reason . . .'.[26] This rule of reason is revealed by history, which manifests the principles of nature by which man lives and to which he must conform. The study of history, therefore, can direct and alter the character of a man; and in this way the misguided motions of evils can be assuaged, diminished or even completely checked. Thus history forms a philosophy of life which conforms man 'to the designs of God manifested in the constitution of human nature . . .'.[27]

This is Bolingbroke's great ideal for history, and after he has established his philosophical Candide in the best of all possible worlds, it is essential to see how this world coincides with the real world. Do historians really fulfil the requisites which he has required of them? If they do not succeed, where and why do they fail? Because Bolingbroke is so much part of his age, he desires to direct and alter the precepts of his own age by means of his philosophy of history. He applies his principles to an age which he despises and to authors whom he distrusts. The results he already knows, but he uses the examples of his own time to underscore the validity of his ideas; in part because others are less enlightened, and in part because many of them still accept the teachings of authorities he knows to be wrong. By demonstrating their faults he upholds his own truths, destroys his opponents and converts the previously ignorant.

He proceeds by making an analysis of ancient history both classical and religious. From these studies he will be able to support the cliché of his time—not that he thinks of it as a cliché—that history really begins with the sixteenth century. However, albeit subscribing to what is a foreshortening of history, Bolingbroke recognises that earlier historians had often made noble efforts and in some cases real contributions. Their contribution is significant because one of the most notable tasks of history is to explain origins and causes. Origins of society are matters which interest all men, for it is natural for them to want to know whence they came. It is a form of national genealogy. Further, by the proper establishment of origins precise chronology may be worked out and events placed in the correct time-sequence to illustrate their correct relationships and to serve as demonstrations in the teaching of history's lessons. Ancient historians failed in these basic tasks; hence their reliability in other areas is open to question.

This conclusion is perhaps not altogether just since the peduncles of time are almost inevitably concealed by later growth. The old historians failed because they did not have adequate sources, although it can be argued the sources existed but they did not know how to use them properly. Fable and myth were substituted, and into these were woven snippets of truth to give verisimilitude to the garment of history. Each historian, having limited factual information, imagined facts to fill the lacunae, and then made up for himself what appeared to be a reasonable picture of the world before his time. He was appealing to passion and imagination and creating precepts or philosophies which could not conform to nature. Because his knowledge of chronology was virtually non-existent, he could at best use only the memory of living men. Since the proper sequence of events in time is one of the first things to be forgotten by the human memory, such facts and true situations as the ancient historians had available were not set in time at all. What they did was to take things out of time, and once this was done history lost its sense of direction and events could not be treated as 'anticipations' of future happenings in the temporal order. History simply became more poetical or artistic; it was incapable of expressing political precepts as opposed to psychological truths. Further, the paucity of factual material meant that each historian could attack the writings of his predecessors, claiming that, as Thucydides said of Herodotus, they merely retold myths and were wide of the mark of truth. The result was that Clio and her patron Olympian Zeus were deserted; pyrrhonism followed. Hence the view that history really began with the sixteenth century.

Assuming that classical antiquity could not undertake the tasks which were put to its historians, was there any source which might provide the necessary explanations demanded by Bolingbroke? Well meaning and, to him, uncritical minds would suggest that the one true authority for all that Bolingbroke sought was the Bible. He takes issue with this view instantly. For him the entire Old Testament can be summarised in one word: Myth. Even though he sees the Jewish scriptures not as one book but as a set of books of varying sorts and varying values, the Old Testament, he considers, cannot be history because by no stretch of the imagination can the authors be thought of as historians. They were the purveyors of 'holy romances' which 'slid into tradition, and tradition became history'. These books were delivered 'on the faith of a superstitious people, among whom the art of pious lying prevailed remarkably'.[28] The Greeks, as knowledgeable as they were, do not confirm the Jewish traditions, even though they 'published at least as many idle traditions of other nations, as they propagated of their own'.[29] (Is this a not very subtle attack on Herodotus?)

Whatever credence, therefore, was given to Jewish history—and this includes also the writings of Josephus—came only after christianity for 'the foundations of this system being laid partly in these histories, and in the prophecies joined to them or inserted in them, christianity has reflected back upon them an authority which they had not before . . .'.[30] To assume that the Old Testament is all divinely inspired and all true is nonsense. Were this to be the case, then the Deity would be hopelessly inconsistent and this is impossible because the Deity is pre-eminently reasonable, and reason is never inconsistent. The Old Testament is interesting, even illuminating, but certainly not a definitive source for our knowledge of the ancient world. The New Testament, on the other hand, Bolingbroke takes to be proved—quite how this occurs he does not say—but it does not on this account authenticate the Old Testament. 'Christ came to fulfil the prophecies; but not to consecrate all the written, any more than the oral, traditions of the Jews.'[31] It is self-evident that Moses and his successors in 'the genealogies and histories of the Old Testament' are incapable of supplying 'sufficient foundations for a chronology from the beginning of time, nor for a universal history'.[32] Indeed, it may even be asserted that those who search for a consistent historical account, either factual or chronological, 'in the books of the Old Testament . . . [expect] to find what the authors of these books, whoever they were, never intended. They are extracts of genealogies, not genealogies; extracts of histories, not histories'.[33]

Moreover, there is for Bolingbroke no store of external and independent evidence to authenticate the Old Testament because 'profane chronology is itself so modern, so precarious, that this help does not reach to the greatest part of that time to which sacred chronology extends',[34] and scholars have further muddled the situation by their activities. Such men have allowed 'profane Chronology' if it confirms sacred writings but not otherwise. This canonises the scriptures but does not prove them; it limits the profane but does not support the sacred; this is an application of the law of evidence to one set of facts while the law of hearsay is permitted to stand in the other. The classical authors are subject to scepticism, the sacred authors to pious superstition. The upshot is that 'neither in profane nor sacred authors [are there] such authentic, clear, distinct, and full accounts of the originals of ancient nations, and of the great events of those ages that are commonly called the first ages, . . . [as to] deserve to go by the name of history, or . . . to afford sufficient materials for chronology and history'.[35]

If history is to have, by reason of its basis in actual experience, that didactic quality which Bolingbroke prizes so highly, and if the strictures he has levelled against the ancient historians are valid, then it is quite obvious that no one will read such histories with any serious purpose. The ancient historians indulged themselves in Bolingbroke's opinion in the writing of a kind of historical novel and in the composing of archaeological orations which may be most interesting and entertaining, but which, if we recollect his views on those who turn to history for such reasons, are too superficial to be worth our study. It is true that, if well told, they may have 'a momentary effect upon the mind, by heating the imagination, surprising the judgment, and affecting strongly the passions',[36] but they are not permanent in their effect.

The beliefs which such fiction is able to impose are so fleeting, and the events described so repugnant to our reason, that only with some external authority may the impressions received be even remotely credible. However, 'reason connives at the innocent fraud of imagination; reason dispenses, in favour of probability, with those strict rules of criticism that she has established to try the truth of fact; but after all she receives these fables as fables; and as such only . . . permits imagination to make the most of them'.[37] Imagination deals in what might have been; history deals in what has been. The authors of these fabulous accounts really 'cannot make the slightest momentary impressions on a mind fraught with knowledge, and void of superstition'.[38] The only possibility that such authors might have of influence is as a result of authority assisted by artifice, and even then it only occurs in a mind clouded with ignorance. 'Nothing less than enthusiasm and phrensy can give credit to such histories.'[39] Kernels of truth may exist but in the vast *mélange* of fiction the truth is indiscernible 'and therefore useless to mankind'.[40]

Is there any truth to the idea, crudely expressed by Henry Ford, that 'history is bunk', or, more gracefully by Voltaire, that 'history is a pack of tricks we play on the dead'? To answer affirmatively is to submit tamely to an unreal proposition. History is real; it is not a highly coloured anecdotal story 'full of sound and fury signifying nothing'; and while its participants may have erred through ignorance and even through malice, this does not lessen the value of proper history. The false history is just not history, and it is this untrue history that gives true history its bad name, even though its falsity can only be detected by historical judgment.

Corrupt history is a direct result of vanity. Dictators have been the worst offenders, for they could not bring themselves to believe, or allow the belief to be current, that all their superiority was not based on provable fact. In non-political history the consequences are not dissimilar; zeal and enthusiasm have blinded men to the truth in their desire to embellish their subjects with a hoary antiquity or with an illustrious *muthos*. The truth will properly be what Voltaire wanted history to be: materials accepted, not with credulity, but only after a critical reading of more than one source. Even then it must be with the use of reason which, after all, is as conformable to nature as history should be, that the historian must decide the credibility of his materials and his facts. This process dissociates the historian from the filiopietistic hagiographer and makes him what we in the twentieth century conceive a historian to be.

By ordered criticism one can find 'true history, which could not be found entire' in any single history, and this 'will command our assent when it is formed with judgment, and represented with candour'.[41] If the materials do not exist for obtaining true history then one must be content with ignorance. Absolute ignorance is much to be preferred to falsehood masquerading as truth. Much care must be taken to avoid the traps and pitfalls laid by the deliberately mendacious, but more must be taken to avoid the falsehoods which result from accident. The former will easily be discovered, the latter less easily so, and will have to be inspected with greater precision if deviation from the norm of actual experience is suspected. Bolingbroke is merely restating a historical criticism that is as old as Herodotus. Suspect the mythological and the fabulous that conflict with human experience; keep an open mind on the sources, especially if they are contradictory; and trust first hand information rather than any other. To Bolingbroke the best history is contemporary history, for here he feels error is less likely to exist. The materials for such history are at hand and can be readily used. In actuality Bolingbroke is most unwise in his preference for contemporary history because contemporary prejudices are destructive of the truth, while the loss of information through antiquity is more than offset by the wisdom and perspective that comes with the passage of time.

Even assuming, then, that there is such a thing as good history, there are so many histories written that the extraction of the truth becomes very difficult. One must use discretion in one's reading otherwise one will only be excessively diligent with no time to be brilliant. Without discrimination one will only collect wheelbarrow-loads of disembodied facts; such 'nuggetry' is the offspring of indiscriminate reading and as such is valueless—mere *nugae* in fact. Anecdotes and keyhole history merely pander to the butterfly philosophers; they contribute only entertainment and nothing 'towards our improvement in wisdom and virtue',[42] and they are as valueless as annals for, like them, they interpret nothing; hence they teach nothing and are therefore not history.

In the company of annalists Bolingbroke places the abridgers who destroy original works and leave only their skeletal remains, and not very complete ones at that. The Romans had annalists who recorded things, but they were never historians. It is only as civilisation develops, bringing with it a sense of time, that history comes into its own. The abridger with his skeleton is taking what passes for history outside of time and consequently has violated the chief element in history, namely, time and therefore has created no history.

In the ancient world the Greeks had historians in Thucydides and Xenophon, but they were the only ones, and even so were very particular historians since they treated for the most part such limited topics. The Greeks had too much 'levity as well as loquacity'[43] to be competent historians. The Romans had historians in Sallust, Livy and Tacitus. They saw the sweep of events, and Livy is particularly to be praised for the use of sources and for his gigantic project of 'one stupendous draught, the whole progress of that government from liberty to servitude'.[44] It is on this universal scale that good history is developed.

Bolingbroke, like his contemporaries and like Voltaire in particular, was vitally concerned with universal history. The learned monograph was unimportant. A statesman's thought should be cast in the mould of the national epic, not in didactic limericks. To see the reason of history, a man must see the whole panorama of events. Vision is impaired by a plethora of petty detail, and it is only on a broad sweep of canvas that the perspective of history can be seen. Here, as elsewhere, Bolingbroke is the true child of his age.

In the course of his life Bolingbroke wrote many things of a decidedly historical nature but to consider him as a 'serious historian' in the modern sense would be a gross error, for he was not and never pretended to be a serious scholar. The writing of history to him was an avocation not a profession; Bolingbroke wrote history as a gentleman in his library putting down his ideas and thoughts in order to explain, through historical studies, his own philosophy of life.

To Bolingbroke, as to most of his contemporaries, the only true history is contemporary history and consequently he has no interest in the classical historians, the medieval chroniclers or their immediate

successors in the renaissance. He dates true history with the commence-
ment of the sixteenth century. However, in his *Remarks on the History
of England* he does give a reasonably long account of England prior to
1485 to provide a prologue or introduction for the period of history
that is to receive his main emphasis. There is in fact a conflict between
the need for historical perspective and extended experience and alter-
nately the dictates of immediate utility. Bolingbroke is, therefore,
compelled by theoretical considerations to set his facts in some perspective, but he does not really think any the more of this early period.
Concerning it he observes:

> To be entirely ignorant of the ages which precede this era [i.e.
> the end of the fifteenth century] would be shameful. Nay some
> indulgence may be had to a temperate curiosity in the review of
> them, but to be learned about them is a ridiculous affectation
> in any man who means to be useful to the present age. Down to
> this era let us read history; from this era, and down to our own
> time, let us study it.[45]

Bolingbroke wrote no history during the years he was in power; he was
too involved in making history. His scholarship was the result of
enforced idleness, not the activity of a man of business. As George
Macaulay Trevelyan so aptly says of Bolingbroke's writings: 'The
reader must remember that he is reading the words not of Henry St
John of 1710–1712, but of . . . a man chastened by long years of proscription and exile, trying to recover by his pen what he had lost by his
actions; a man purged by a long penance.'[46]

It is not, therefore, surprising to find that his history is largely past
politics. However, there are other forces which are observed by him
even if only superficially. He is interested in economics, geography and
personalities, though all of these—and there will be more elucidation of
these points later—are but incidental to the main theme.

Bolingbroke's historical writings fall into two main categories: one
concerned with European history, the other with English history. His
European histories are all very similar in style, scope and direction;
they are designed to endorse the sensible policies of Bolingbroke and
his party with a special emphasis on the Peace of Utrecht. His English
histories are written to demonstrate the dangers of court favourites (for
this read Walpole) and in factions (for this read the whigs). There are in
addition some minor historical writings but these merely underscore

the ideas found elsewhere. For example, in his *On the Policy of the Athenians* he equates Walpole with Pericles who had 'by the licentious distribution of bribes and bounties amongst the people, soon extinguished all sentiments of their former honesty and love of country'.[47] In all probability he means to compare himself in the same work to the 'good Aristides'.

The *Letters on the Study and Use of History* are in part philosophical and in part historical commentary. Letters I to V give Bolingbroke's ideas on history and historical criticism; Letters VI to VIII—and by far the longer part of the series—are similar, but in a more complete form, to the ideas expressed in his *Plan for a General History of Europe*. It is possible that Letters VII and VIII were not originally part of the series *Letters on the Study and Use of History*, but were the only part of Bolingbroke's general history to be written. As the whole of the general history was never completed it may well be that Bolingbroke simply tacked on the Letters VII and VIII to round out his *Letters on the Study and Use of History*. Although the *Letters on the Study and Use of History* was actually published prior to his *Plan for a General History of Europe*, there is no proof that composition took place in that order; most of Bolingbroke's works were written for private circulation long before they were published.

In Letter VI he gives a general survey of the state of Europe at the beginning of the sixteenth century. He presents a sensible and reasoned account of the causes of the Reformation and a solid and perceptive narrative of the rise of the national monarchies. His concepts of causality, while in many ways crude, show a discernment which, considering the age in which he wrote, i.e. before the rise of modern historical criticism, is highly original and commendable. In his account of the rise of the modern state, for example, he is concerned to emphasise the significance of the concept of the balance of power. His interest here, however, is largely coloured by his later explanations of his own role during the negotiations and settlement of the Peace of Utrecht. In all, he emphasises that the 'thread of history that you [Lord Cornbury, to whom the letters were ostensibly written] are to keep, is that of the nations who are and must always be concerned in the same scenes of action with your own'.[48] In other words, one does not have to bother with the history of some remote society whose history does not directly influence one's national history. For example, according to Bolingbroke's view, it would be rather pointless to be excessively concerned with the history of Tibet in the sixteenth century as it has little or no direct connection with England. Hence, all of his historical thinking is directed towards western Europe.

Having set out his historical stage with care, he proceeds to give in more detail the history of the rise of France as the predominant power in Europe, and of the concomitant and resultant dangers. France was *the* enemy for Bolingbroke; Spain and Austria, by the time he seriously considers history to have begun, are already on the decline or, if not yet obsolescent, certainly containing within them the seeds of their later collapse. Bolingbroke is extremely critical of English policy from the time of Cromwell until the accession of William III. The reign of Charles II is disgraceful, a disaster resulting from favourites and from faction—the mistresses and the Cabal—and the dismissal of the one true statesman, Lord Clarendon. He sees in Clarendon almost the *beau-idéal* of his patriot who stands above faction and in consequence is sacrificed when men of little minds and no virtue assume power. But the real hero for Bolingbroke is William of Orange because he led the coalition against France, and did so with sense and realism. To Bolingbroke William's policies represented sanity and true patriotism. (It must be noted, however, that he had not always felt this way; he had been a party to the attacks on William's ministers after the signing of the Partition Treaties.) True patriotism, he considers, and sensible government, with a due emphasis on the balance of power, were only fully restored when he himself was in office directing affairs, and when the Peace of Utrecht provided the natural conclusion to William's plans. He is quite aware that the treaty was a partisan measure but he feels, and here he is probably right, that the whigs opposing the signing of the treaty had completely lost sight of reality in their desire to continue the war long after its aims had been achieved.

Bolingbroke knew, and so did his opponents in their saner moments, that the purpose of the war was to ensure that neither France nor Austria should dominate the European scene, and that the Spanish inheritance should be partitioned among the several claimants. The king of Spain was less dangerous than an Austrian hegemony or an enlarged sphere of influence for Louis XIV. The Treaty of Utrecht was not perfect, but it did at least satisfy the basic requirements for a European settlement. Errors there were, but it was as good as it could be made. This is all special pleading of course, but it does express a view of the events which is quite acceptable to any but the most biased supporter of the whig tradition. It is also a view that must receive careful consideration from any thoughtful historian.

In his *Remarks on the History of England*, which appeared originally in the *Craftsman*, it is evident almost from the first page that this work is designed to be not so much a historical study as we think of such a study but rather as a savage attack on the existing government. To Bolingbroke this is not a contradiction because he is using history as he would claim it should be used: namely, to teach by example. Therefore it will be immediately apparent that the didactic quality of history is meant to predominate, and the facts will be selected in such a way as may best demonstrate the truth as Bolingbroke sees it. There is no attempt to be unbiased. Manning's unjustifiably savage description of Newman can be justly applied to Bolingbroke; he was assuredly 'a great hater', and he wrote in a correspondingly vitriolic fashion against his opponents.

As in his survey of European history, he sets out to give the general background, emphasising where possible incidents and situations that could apply directly to his case. He makes it clear that here too his real interest in history does not begin until the reign of Henry VII, although many of his villains and his examples of the dangers of faction are to be found in the pre-Tudor period. Throughout the entire work clear parallels are drawn between Walpole, the favourite of the moment, and earlier prototypes. Mortimer, Buckingham, and especially Wolsey are taken and studied as illustrations of the rapacious, cunning and tyrannical despoilers of liberty, whose successors, once they themselves are known through history's teachings, can be forestalled and deposed. It is a case of applying knowledge to experience: by learning from the past one can direct events in the present and in the future.

In the course of his historical writings Bolingbroke emphasises the role and influence of 'faction' in history. A faction may be defined as a group which is concerned exclusively for its own welfare—be this economic, social or political. One might add that the members of a faction see all methods to be good, not necessarily virtuous, but acceptable if they serve the ends of faction. To a faction its own welfare is the sole reason for its existence, and all of its activities must be subordinated to this end. A faction destroys in order to govern, and, as Bolingbroke says, the inevitable outcome of such activities is a diminution of freedom and liberty. Faction cannot help being a tyrant when its raison d'être is solely the promotion of its own policies. It was the great evil of the past, and only when the sovereign subdued faction could there be government for the people as a whole. Bolingbroke is well aware that sovereigns also can be involved in factions; they are, as history demonstrates in the misfortunes of Richard II and Charles I, as evil as factions aimed directly against the people, for faction in any guise limits the liberty of the people.

This account of English history is also used by Bolingbroke to explain what the government or constitution is, and how it works. His thesis is best summarised in his own words:

> A king of Great Britain is that supreme magistrate who has a negative voice in the legislature. He is entrusted with the executive power, and several other powers and privileges, which we call prerogatives, are annexed to this trust. The two houses of parliament have their rights and privileges; some of which are common to both, others particular to each. They prepare, they pass bills, or they refuse to pass such as are sent to them. They address, represent, advise, remonstrate. The supreme judicature resides in the lords. The commons are the grand inquest of the nation ... If the legislative as well as the executive power, was wholly in the king, as in some countries, he would be absolute; if in the lords, our government would be an aristocracy; if in the commons, a democracy. It is this division of power, these distinct privileges attributed to the king, to the lords, and to the commons, which constitute a limited monarchy.[49]

In other words he sees the government of England as consisting of a division of power designed to effect a stable equilibrium. When one or more parts of the government claim excessive power then liberty is curtailed and the other parts must combine to redress the balance. History shows that when the sovereign has overcome faction and reigns as he ought then the state is in perfect balance. And it is from seeing in history examples of the disruption of society, but also more from seeing examples of the virtuous society, that we can direct our attention and policies for the future.

There was one age when the sovereign ruled as Bolingbroke would have all sovereigns rule; this was the Elizabethan age. To him, the zenith of English history was attained with the reign of Queen Elizabeth, and her reign was truly a golden age. She was, for Bolingbroke, the ideal monarch.

> She was wise enough to see clearly into the nature of ... government ... to know that 'the supreme head of ... such a government owes a supreme service to the whole.' She was

wise enough to know that to be powerful she must either usurp on her people, deceive them or gain them. The first two, she saw, were hard, dangerous and dishonourable. The last, she saw, was easy, safe and glorious. . . . She made herself very soon the most popular person in the kingdom. In her reign, the sense of the court, the sense of parliament and the sense of the people were the same; and whenever she exerted her own strength, she exerted the strength of the whole nation. . . . She threw herself entirely on the affections of her subjects, . . . she seemed to decline all other tenure of the crown. . . . The being not only tied, but knit to her people was her aim; and she pursued this great point of view on all occasions; the least, as well as the greatest; . . . and when she courted her people, she courted them like a queen. This popularity was sometimes carried so far . . . that her enemies endeavoured to make it pass for gross and fulsome affection . . . It might have shocked, instead of alluring; if it had not been seconded by every action of her life, and contradicted by none.[50]

It is evident that such lavish praise as this is but a prelude to a long and intense discussion of this golden age, a dissertation which is one long pæan of praise for the 'bright Occidental star'. She succeeded because she knew how to rule; she 'was supported by the spirit of liberty' and hence ought to be reckoned the true example of English sovereignty. In short, one might well say that Bolingbroke wanted 'Back to Elizabeth' to be the fundamental plank of his political platform. Furthermore, he hoped to use the reign of Elizabeth, the example par excellence of how a sovereign should govern, as a foil for the failures of the Stuarts. The purpose was to indicate that the best reading matter that the House of Hanover could take up would be the accounts of the reign of Elizabeth, and that if the House of Hanover read its history properly it too might receive the plaudits of posterity. If, however, its members failed to read their history and continued as prisoners of faction, then they would fail as surely as the Stuarts. Let the true patriots return and drive out the money changers; let Bolingbroke and Co. take over the business and throw out Walpole and his gang, and then at last all would be well. History would confirm these conclusions without any difficulty.

Although Bolingbroke's history is largely written from the political viewpoint, he does not ignore the value of commerce, which was good in the Elizabethan age because stock-jobbery had not become rampant. He is also in his way something of a geopolitician: 'An island under one government, advantageously situated, rich in itself, richer by its commerce, can have no necessity, in the ordinary course of affairs, to take up the policy of the continent, to enter into the system of alliances ... or, in short, to act any other part than that of a friendly neighbour and fair trader.'[51] Here is a good apology for splendid isolation. His attitude to the continent would find a ready echo in the twentieth century: 'Our nation inhabits an island ... we must take the advantages of this situation ... we must always remember that we are not part of the continent, but we must never forget that we are neighbours to it.'[52] England's prosperity and strength came from its situation. Bolingbroke stresses that the navy must be kept at full strength, and he insists that the French are the true enemies of the country. Considering that he was vilified for his presumedly francophile policy and for his dismantling of England's defences, this protestation of his patriotism may seem false. But we must remember Trevelyan's comment that this was written in the calm of afterthought when different circumstances existed, not when the events themselves were being enacted and when party passions were at their highest pitch.

An historian's sources are sometimes a good indication of his reliability. Bolingbroke in his *Remarks &c.* uses good secondary material and excellent primary sources. Among the latter were Lord Clarendon's *History of the Rebellion and Civil Wars in England* and Bishop Burnet's *History of My Own Times*, and among the former William Camden's *Britannia* and *Annales Rerum Anglicarum* (this possibly was his source for the reign of Elizabeth), Nathaniel Bacon's *An Historical Discourse of the Laws and Government of England &c.*, Francis Bacon's *The History of the Reign of King Henry the Seventh*, and Paul de Rapin's *The History of England*. Of all of these works Rapin is the most frequently cited, and it obviously provided him with his most complete account of English history. The use of such sources indicates an awareness of the importance of adequate materials for the writing of good history. He therefore acquits himself of the accusations which he levels at the historians of antiquity for their inadequate use of sources. For his *Letters &c.* he cites very frequently Pierre Bayle's *Dictionnaire Historique et Critique* which was the best available work at the time. Other authors cited or referred to are Herodotus, Thucydides, Cicero, Caesar, Livy, Josephus, Machiavelli, Guicciardini and Bodin. Whether Bolingbroke did his own research is open to question. It is quite possible that he had some assistance, but during his retirement from parliament in the years 1708 to 1710 and in his long years of banishment he had much time for reading. It is not inconceivable that he may therefore have read many of these authors carefully, even if he had not read them all with equal attention. Considering, therefore, that he was not a professional scholar and that he probably never examined original documents, one can justifiably say that Bolingbroke shows in his choice of materials a real sense of discrimination and judgment.

One of Bolingbroke's greatest assets is his superb style; he has a sense of both majesty and epigram. Consider such examples as the following on the state of the church just prior to the Reformation: 'The magicians themselves broke the charm by which they had bound mankind for so many ages'; and 'the adventure of that knight-errant, who, thinking himself happy in the arms of a celestial nymph, found that he was the miserable slave of an infernal hag';[53] or 'the horrid crimes of Alexander VI, the saucy ambition of Julius II, the immense profusion and scandalous exactions of Leo X'.[54] Bolingbroke's portrait of James I would have done credit to a Macaulay or a Trevelyan:

> Fraught with learning, not with knowledge; ignorant of the true principles of government; more a stranger to our constitution by his notions and habits of thinking, than to our country by his birth; obstinate, though not steady; misled by self opinion, and confirmed in error by superlative pedantry, King James the First seemed to expect the love, and to demand the obedience of his subjects, purely because the crown had dropped on his head.[55]

But Bolingbroke must be read to gain the full pleasure of his writings. The whole is like a great velvet cloak bespangled with brilliants and baubles; sometimes it is false or excessive but it is always magnificent.

It is in Letter V that Bolingbroke's views on history are most aptly stated, and give perhaps the best illustration of him as an historian.

> Man is the subject of every history; and to know him well we must see him and consider him, as history alone can present him to us, in every age, in every country, in every state, in life and in death. History therefore of all kinds, of civilized and uncivilized, of ancient and modern nations, in short all history that descends to a sufficient detail of human actions and characters, is useful to bring us acquainted with our species, nay with

ourselves. To teach and to inculcate the general principles of virtue, and the general rules of wisdom and good policy, which result from such details of actions and characters, comes for the most part, and always should come, expressly and directly into the design of those who are capable of giving such details; and therefore whilst they narrate as historians, they hint often as philosophers, they put into our hands as it were, on every proper occasion, the end of a clue that serves to remind us of searching, and to guide us in the search of that truth which the example before us either establishes or illustrates. If a writer neglects this part, we are able however to supply his neglect by our own attention and industry, and when he gives us a good history of Peruvians, or Mexicans, of Chinese or Tartars, of Muscovites or Negroes, we may blame him, but we must blame ourselves much more, if we do not make it a good lesson of philosophy. This being the general use of history, it is not to be neglected. Every one may make it who is able to read and to reflect on what he reads, and every one who makes it will find in his degree the benefit that arises from an early acquaintance contracted in this manner with mankind. We are not only passangers or sojourners in this world, but we are absolute strangers at the first steps we make in it. Our guides are often ignorant, often unfaithful. By this map of the country which history spreads before us, we may learn, if we please, to guide ourselves. In our journey through it we are beset on every side. We are besieged sometimes even in our strongest holds. Terrors and temptations, conducted by the passions of other men, assault us, and our passions that correspond with these, betray us. History is a collection of the journals of those who have travelled through the same country and been exposed to the same accidents, and their good and ill success are equally instructive. In this pursuit of knowledge an immense field is spread before us: general histories, sacred and profane; the histories of particular countries, particular events, particular orders, particular men; memorials, anecdotes, travels. But we must not ramble in this field without discernment or choice, nor even with these must we ramble too long.[56]

On Religion and
Philosophy

I am deep in a world that is very entertaining; or rather the demolitions of
the metaphysical world; which that intellectual Sampson of Battersea has
pulled down about our ears: but with the difference, that here the Philistine
is the Hero and the poor Saints are crushed. I have gone through the *Essay
on Human Knowledge* and will confess that fine as it is and irresistible as the
vogue for writings of that kind may be, I cannot think it the greatest per-
formance that ever was, as I had been made to expect. Old matter new
dressed and often tawdry enough....

WILLIAM PITT, Earl of Chatham

THE history of thought recounts numerous controversies which
arose after a scholarly thesis had been exposed to public consideration. But these controversies seem to belong to the
more distant past, and hence it often surprises us to discover
that many speculative writings of the eighteenth century were regarded
as controversial by contemporaries, for to us today they seem so
'reasonable' as to be commonplace, simply because we have accepted
and taken for granted the results of those controversies. One is all too
prone to see the eighteenth century as the *Aufklärung*, and to regard the
sentiments of the enlightened as the unanimous verdict of society. In
fact, what we see are only the sentiments of the age's most brilliant and
witty spokesmen. Then, as now, the intellectuals stood apart from the

Weltanschauung of the age, while the great mass of society was unadapt-able and conservative and was as suspicious of new ideas as any generally uneducated group can be. It is not surprising that popular reaction to Bolingbroke's criticisms of christianity were violent. Although many people may have doubted the verbal inspiration of the sacred scrip-tures, there was no general approbation for an onslaught on the traditional chart of religion. Bolingbroke's temerity was met with universal execration when his philosophical and religious tracts were published. None of his religious writings appeared before his death, for he had rightly estimated the sentimentality of society, even though this was often hidden beneath an icing of rationalism, and had kept his subversive and critical ideas to himself or imparted them only to a very select group of friends.

Bolingbroke's religious and philosophical writings are all of a piece. They have the common aim of clearing away the jungle of myth and superstition in religion and philosophy, and of erecting an elegant and precise system of his own.[1] His aims were not particularly new or original, since many others have undertaken to clean the Augean stables of philosophy and religion, to carry out the socratic elenchus or to fulfil the command of Jeremiah to root out and pull down. But it was the vehemence of his attacks, the brilliance of his exposition and the amazing and contradictory attitudes which he struck that were astounding. The overall effect was that his contemporaries were appalled; but if they had recollected his career, its strengths and its weaknesses, they would have found them reflected in his writings. As in politics, so in religion, he failed, in spite of his skill and brilliance, to convert many to his ideas: ideas which had more heat than light, more ingenuity in their conception than validity in their exposition, and more elegance in their phraseology than depth in their meaning. Nevertheless his writings have a double significance. First, they are one of the best examples of the eighteenth-century intellect in action; and secondly, they attempt to establish a set of rational precepts for religion which would withstand the criticism of later ages even less inclined to superstition than his own. That the attempt did not succeed does not mean that it is without value, for all experiments lead man to a greater understanding of the truth, even if that understanding lies in a reaction against the experiment. One such reaction, that of William Blake, may help to put Bolingbroke into perspective. 'Your Religion, O Deists! is the worship of the God of this world by the means of what you call natural religion and natural philosophy, and of natural morality or self-righteousness, the selfish virtues of the natural heart. This was the religion of the Pharisees who murder'd Jesus. Deism is the same and ends in the same.'[2]

Bolingbroke said that he was not an atheist; although he said many things apparently to the contrary, it seems reasonable to assume that in disavowing atheism he was being truthful. He accepted the existence of God, and in the *Letters to M. De Pouilly* written in 1720 he proves to his own satisfaction, through the concept of a continuous creation counter-acting the disintegration of the forces of the natural order, that the world must owe its existence and survival to a creator.

In human experience it is difficult to conceive that matter is not eternal and that things have not always been much as they now are. 'The same nature, and the same course of things, that exist actually, have always existed.'[3] This might seem to reduce God to the rôle of the Demiurge, but in fact it points to the coexistence of creator and creation. If the world is thereby eternal and in some sense self-existent, it is by definition the only eternal: everything that exists must have a cause 'either out of itself, or in itself'; but the only eternal has no 'cause of its existence out of itself' and must exist entirely 'by the necessity of its own nature'.[4] What is meant by the phrase 'necessity of its own nature'? If it has no meaning then there is no eternity, but if there is a first cause and the world is a creation, then it may partake in the eternal necessity of the first cause. Now this first cause may not be 'God', but it is definitely something and once the something is accepted it might be God. Having declared that he accepts that God is this first cause, Bolingbroke has *ipso facto* established for himself the necessary existence of God. In one of his occasional pieces, *A Letter on One of Archbishop Tillotson's Sermons*, he says very specifically and explicitly: 'There is a God, a first intelligent Cause of all things, whose infinite wisdom and power appear in all His works.'[5] In saying this he did not advocate what he called the fictions of 'theistical poets, philosophers and legislators'[6] who have conjured up a number of explanations for the first principles and the operations of divine powers. There are no hypothetical worlds as advocated by these artistic naturalists: there is only one actual and existent world, eternal because God is eternal.

He argued 'from the intuitive knowledge of ourselves, and the sensitive knowledge of objects exterior to ourselves, which we have, up to that demonstrative knowledge of God's existence, which we are able to acquire by due use of our reason'.[7] There are two points to be made here. First, that Bolingbroke recognises the rôle of the supra-sensible in converting sense-data into intelligible perceptions. A refutation of this would in fact deny all 'sensitive knowledge', because 'sensitive knowledge' cannot in itself bring knowledge of 'inward constitutions of substances and their real essences'.[8] Sensitive knowledge does not, on the other hand, deny existence. Secondly, this passage illustrates Bolingbroke's one-sided view of the relationship between natural and revealed theology. He accepts only what Aquinas calls the first half of the tension between 'an ascent by the natural light of reason through created things to the knowledge of God', and 'a descent by the mode of revelation of divine truth which exceeds the human intellect . . . not demonstrated to our sight but delivered for our belief'.[9]

Bolingbroke denies the validity of revelation on the ground that it is unnecessary since nature supplies what is necessary in all instances. The law of nature is perfect, and this perfection is such that it has never shown any need of further elaboration by revelation. Neglecting the origins of the criteria by which he judges 'nature', he exalts the general laws of nature at the expense of individual insight. 'God has not made any particular systems, nor established particular providences for particular nations, much less for particular men, as far as we can discover by the help of reason and experience.'[10] But because men seem to have a peculiar penchant for revelation either personal or vicarious, and because they refuse to surrender this belief even when reason and experience seem to indicate the contrary, Bolingbroke is willing to accept for the moment this general belief. He implies that he is willing to accept the idea of revelation, but he totally rejects the arguments presented for it; his view is that the arguments given in defence of revelation are specious but the idea of it is not necessarily so.

This is pure casuistry, of course, but jesuitical argument was never far from Bolingbroke at any time. He is willing to predicate revelation of all knowledge, but is unwilling, in common with his age, to accept the intrusive element of a higher revelation by which his natural theology or objectified revelation may be judged. He ignores that 'once a thing has been revealed it can be shown to be "conformable to right reason", but it cannot therefore be said that reason alone could prove it—that surely is to name a *vaticinium ex eventu*. What is more, all knowledge may come within the circle of revelation, but that circle can only be meaningful with the revelation of its centre.'[11] By discarding the specious arguments for the truth of revelation, Bolingbroke considers that 'revelation' will be acceptable, and by analogy he will be able to be a christian for, once this great stumbling-block is discarded, christianity and Bolingbroke's true natural religion are one.

While accepting in general the concept of revelation, though not the specific arguments for it, he totally disallows Old Testament revelation. Here he could be said to be on safer ground, since the Old Testament is essentially a *praeparatio evangelica*, and the christian tends to base his belief on the New Testament. Criticism of the Old Testament does not really do too much to alarm the orthodox, and Bolingbroke considers that it would be reasonable to discard it entirely except for the prophetic indications of the coming messiah in which it is necessary to christianity. The message of Jesus, in his view, did not supplement Moses or fulfil the law, but rather began a new canon of belief that was not dependent on the mosaic tradition. Moses is singled out for particular attack. He was 'ignorant of the true system of the universe',[12] and, if really appointed by God to write for posterity, he should not have been content with writing simply about 'one God, the Creator of all things'.[13] As a divinely inspired author, Moses should have given an irrefutable demonstration 'that his history might answer all the designs of eternal wisdom, it should have been proportioned to the ignorance of the Israelites . . . without giving so much reason to people, better informed, to believe him as ignorant as any uninspired person could be'.[14] Moses, in fact, is criticised for his lack of a philosophy, with which Bolingbroke seeks to support religion.

A comparison might be made with some early christian apologists who endeavoured to translate the christian faith in terms of Greek philosophy, believing as they did that 'philosophy', as one of their number Clement of Alexandria said, 'was necessary to the Greeks to bring them to righteousness . . . for philosophy educated the Greek world as the law did the Hebrews to bring them to Christ'. Bolingbroke's philosophy is not, according to him, out of phase with true christianity, any more than Plato was out of phase with true christianity; the only difficulty is to persuade mankind who have been led into error to see this fact. Christianity has been perverted and Bolingbroke intends to restore it.

In his *Letters to M. De Pouilly* he gives as his basis for deciding what is true or false, the following categories of fact. First, the fact verifiable by experiment and therefore probable to the highest degree. Second, the fact repugnant to experience but accepted on authority.

The authority naturally must be such that there can be practically no doubt of the rightness of the views presented. Third, the fact which is frequent and notorious but not in our experience. Fourth, the fact which exists in experience but has no duplicates and no contradictions. Fifth, the fact which is conformable to experience by analogy. Lastly, the fact of which there are no examples, but to deny the existence of it is to state an absurdity. According to him the mosaic writings cannot be accepted because they cannot be assigned to any of these categories of historical fact.[15] (The failure of Moses to qualify as an historian has already been mentioned in chapter 2, page 57 and will be referred to again presently.)

What is more, facts have to be supported by a variety of proofs, and in the absence of such proofs grave doubt can be cast on their probability—although excessive remoteness in time may alter the case, and what is only in consequence of this a relative proof may be acceptable as giving relative probability to a fact.

> Common sense requires that everything proposed to the understanding, should be accompanied with such proofs as the nature of it can furnish. He who requires more, is guilty of absurdity. He who requires less, of rashness. As the nature and the proposition decides, what proofs are exigible and what not, so the kind of proof determines the class into which the proposition is to be ranged. He, for instance, who affirms that there is a God, advances a proposition which is an object of demonstrative knowledge alone, and a demonstration is required from him. If he makes the demonstration, we are obliged to own that we know there is a God, and the proposition becomes a judgment of nature, not merely an opinion, according to the distinctions made somewhere in Tully; tho' demonstrations are sometimes called opinions, as opinions are often called demonstrations. If, by his fault or by ours, we have not a clear perception of the ideas or of the connection of them which form this demonstration, or if, without troubling ourselves to follow it, we receive the proposition for true on the authority of others, it is, indeed, opinion, not knowledge in us. But whether we receive it, or whether we reject it, we can neither require nor employ, with propriety, any other proofs than those which are conformable to the nature of the proposition. Tradition is not one of them. It may prove that men have

generally believed in God, but it cannot prove that such a Being exists. Nothing can be more trifling, therefore to insist, as theists are apt to do, on this proof, as if the opinion proved the fact; as if all men had been alike capable of the demonstration; or, as if the demonstration was not necessary to establish the truth of the opinion. Demonstration, indeed, is not necessary on the hypothesis, that all men have an innate idea of God. But this hypothesis has been, I think, long exploded. I do not remember, at least to have it maintained by more than one archbishop, two or three ignorant monks, and as many devout ladies.[16]

It is not essential to give here a detailed review of Bolingbroke's criticisms of mosaic writings and of historical proof in general. (See chapter 2.) It need only be said that in accordance with his notion of a general law of nature excluding individual inspiration, he takes the lack of independent testimony for the mosaic account of Creation and the Fall as proof of its impossibility. He attempts to show that the accounts written by Moses of the history of the world are simply not corroborated anywhere else, but he is not entirely consistent in this attempt since he recognises that all civilisations account in their histories for the beginning of creation in a fashion not dissimilar to that used by Moses. If, moreover, Bolingbroke had truly searched, or had been able to search, through ancient records, he would have found certain corroborations of the first five books of the Old Testament. As he places so much emphasis on reason and on the value of independent testimony, it would have been impossible for him not to have given some acknowledgement of the validity of the mosaic writings. As it is he sweeps any cavils aside with the statement that on every page there 'are gross defects, and palpable falsehoods . . . and the whole tenor of them is such as no man, who acknowledges a supreme, all perfect Being, can believe it to be His word',[17] and goes on to say that the 'testimony of Moses cannot be reputed an historical testimony, if we give no more credit to him than we should give to any other historian' and that we cannot 'admit his testimony, for divine, without absurdity and blasphemy'.[18] The whole is improbable and opposed to experience; it is so many 'tales that would appear fit to amuse children alone'.[19] What is worse, it sanctifies 'pagan rites and ceremonies in theological language' and profanes 'the pure worship of God'.[20] Moses is not acceptable as an historian because he is too credulous, and if he is unreliable in his factual presentation he is even more so in his theological or extra-factual accounts. Mosaic revelation is inadmissible.

Bolingbroke therefore has demolished mosaic revelation, and by so doing has attacked the foundations of all revelation. He has, in short, 'rejected any revelation which was not accompanied by miraculous evidence for want of authority, and any which was so accompanied for want of probability'.[21] However, this does not mean that he denies the christian religion. In fact, he says of the latter that

> 'no religion ever appeared in the world, whose natural tendency was so much directed to promote the peace and happiness of mankind. If it has had a contrary effect, it has had it apparently, not really. . . . Christianity is founded on the universal law of nature . . . the gospel teaches the great and fundamental prin-ciple of this law, universal benevolence recommends the precepts of it, and commends the observation of them in par-ticular instances occasionally, always supposes them, always enforces them, and makes the law of right reason a law in every possible definition of the word beyond all cavil. . . . Christianity, genuine Christianity, is contained in the gospels, it is the word of God, it requires, therefore, our veneration, and a strict con-formity to it.'[22]

These are statements that could hardly be considered unorthodox, and the fact that christianity could evoke such sentiments illumines its ability to win universal approbation even in the hardened rationalism of the eighteenth century. Bolingbroke's sentiments may express true christianity, but it is not, he considers, true christianity which is being taught to society. Lucifer's emissaries, the theologians, have appeared and have dissected and distorted the gospel teachings. 'Theology is in fault, not religion. Theology is a science that may be compared justly to the box of Pandora. Many good things lie uppermost in it. But many evil lie under them, and scatter plagues and desolation through the world.'[23]

The gospels alone are acceptable. The New Testament 'is in truth the system of natural religion, and such it might have continued to the unspeakable advantage of mankind, if it had been propagated with the same simplicity with which it was originally taught by Christ him-self'.[24] Unfortunately this did not occur, and distortions of the *ipsissima verba* of Christ appeared almost immediately. Christians ought to have accepted the message as it was given and not tried to explain it, for 'explanations in all these cases serve only to multiply disputes, on human, instead of divine authority'.[25] Bolingbroke would agree with the Cambridge Platonists that, although there was much room for controversy *about* religion, religion itself was clear and certain. The man most guilty of introducing explanation and controversy was Saint Paul, whose ideas were a combination of 'oral tradition, cabalistic mysteries, and scraps of Pythagorician, Platonic, and even Stoican doctrines'.[26] He was, moreover, one who had 'a great deal of that assuming air which is apt to accompany much learning, or the opinion of it'.[27]

A return to the gospels will undo all the mischief of Saint Paul, and once more there will be found a 'plain system of belief and practice, fitted for all times, and proportioned to all understandings'.[28] There must be an uncompromising rejection of other writings which are but 'an intricate and dark system ... that casts no light on the rest'.[29] Bolingbroke avows that even Locke, who has given 'an air of coherence, consistency and rationality'[30] to the pauline writings, cannot really unravel the skein of his esoteric formulae. The gospels and the gospels alone have Christ's teachings, which are good; all else is but a series of glosses by theologians making the simple obscure, the natural unnatural, and the straightforward complicated.

It must be observed that, in accepting the gospels, one cannot avoid belief in revelation, but this does not seem to trouble Bolingbroke at all. Initially, of course, he had objected to revelation as something unnecessary and therefore non-existent. Revelation, he held, was contrary to the law of nature, and therefore it had never existed. Yet christianity, which is revelational, is acceptable and is held to conform to the law of nature; and so it is logical to assume that revelation must exist as well. This apparent inconsistency does not seem to have occurred to Bolingbroke, or if it did he studiously avoided a problem discussion of which would have damaged so many of his nicely established theorems.

Having lulled his critics by his seeming orthodoxy, he now moves into a position from which he can attack the universal authority of christianity itself. He starts by declaring that christianity has made no original contributions to the history of thought. Its basic ideology could be found in the writings of the classical Greek philosophers before the appearance of Christ. Platonism, he observes, was established in the Jewish religion, and with it came the 'doctrines of the immortality of the soul, of a future state of rewards and punishments, and even that of a metempsychosis'.[31] All these doctrines are considered by the orthodox christian to be original but they are in fact merely a Greek philosophical addendum to mosaic theology. All that the christians did was to extend these Greek philosophical precepts more widely. One wonders how Bolingbroke would have dealt with the attitude of the primitive church itself, for example in Tertullian's question: 'What has Athens to do with Jerusalem?' His criticism, of course, is far from original, since as early as the fourth century we find Julian the Apostate complaining that christianity has grafted his beloved hellenism on to a Hebrew stock. Having assumed a relationship between the two, Bolingbroke pretends to be astonished that the early christians were so desirous of deriving their own theology from classical philosophy. He even suggests that the grossest of forgeries have been perpetrated in order to give verisimilitude to the claim of christianity that it is supported by classical authority. Actually, the search for authorities, he observes, was entirely unnecessary when all that was needed could be found in Plato, who is 'a sufficient repository of the logical fables and symbols, and of metaphysical mysteries'.[32]

The logical implications of this line of argument, although never explicitly stated, are that the gospels are merely a restatement of the 'theology of Plato', and not, as might have been previously suggested, a restatement of the law of nature, unless one assumes that the former is in accord with the latter. As Plato is portrayed as 'a man whose passion for courtesans, and handsome boys, inspired [him] ... to write ... lewd verses',[33] it is hardly possible that his teachings could be in accord with the sublime law of nature. To Bolingbroke, Plato is not a friend to truth but rather the seducer of the intellect, diverting the innocent from truth to falsehood.

To expect consistency in Bolingbroke's religious ideas is impossible. He seeks to remove theological foundation stones and yet wishes to defend the City of God; and, in spite of his apparent assertions to the contrary, the gospels are not treated as repositories of false doctrines. 'Genuine Christianity was taught by God. Theological Christianity is a religion that men have invented. . . .'[34] Bolingbroke sits in judgment like a latter-day Marcion, retaining what appeals to reason and excising what he finds incomprehensible. It is this perverted christianity that contains the platonic teachings. Plato had postulated some of 'the wildest hypotheses ... [which passed] for systems of sublime knowledge', though at the same time 'he blundered on some divine truths that were not quite beyond human apprehension'.[35] The latter were repeated in the gospels and had value, the former were repeated and expanded and unduly influenced the New Testament, creating a system which denied the law of nature. 'No man ever dreamed so wildly as this author [Plato] writ.'[36] The theologians 'applied Platonic philosophy to introduce and explain Christian, and the authority of Plato to confirm what they received for true on the authority of Christ. They added the epistles to the gospels, the doctrines of Paul to those of Christ; and to all of these, the reveries of heathen philosophy, Rabbinical extravagance, and Christian enthusiasm.'[37] One would have thought that platonic confirmation of christian truth would have supplied the corroboration that Bolingbroke desired for Moses but deemed lacking. In this case, however, he considers that the result was a religion far from the truth and far from the law of nature.

Bolingbroke was not always clear in his thinking; theology was for him a morass of contradictions and inconsistencies, but in elaborating his own views he had fallen prey to many of the evils that, with cavalier amateurism, he had ascribed to theology. It is clear that he accepted God, and he seems to have accepted the gospels, although believing them to err in their repetition of platonic precepts. He is critical of all theologians, beginning with Saint Paul, and seems to reject any idea that is inconsistent with the natural light of reason. Therefore, he appears to discard trinitarianism, for which he finds no support in his two opponents Moses or Plato, and which he thinks antithetical to the teachings of Christ. He is obdurate in his opposition to specific revelation, contending that it violates the law of nature and that this law could not be violated with impunity by anyone wishing to commend his beliefs to men of reason. The 'law of nature' becomes a consensory sanction for what is generally accepted, and covers a multitude of theological sins. Because of many incongruities in his argument, because of a sophisticated pride in his own reason, and because he was not well versed in the sphere which he undertook to attack, his general criticism of religion is not very convincing.

Bolingbroke was always better in attack than in defence, in destruction than construction, and consequently his own system, while well enough stated, is less plausible than the system which he undertook to demolish. As stated earlier, he accepts, apparently without question, that God exists, and he provides a positive demonstration of this, or rather what he denominates as a positive demonstration. If this demonstration can show that God is, then Bolingbroke's initial proposition is no longer his opinion but is a judgment of nature. He refuses to accept the argument from the *consensus gentium*, namely, that all people seem to affirm a belief in a god or gods, that therefore God exists. Instead he reverts to his view that the world is not of itself eternal, and that if so it must have had a creator. The cause of the world order was God, and to reject the existence of such a God whose prime function is to impart order and system and thus intelligibility to the world, is to reject 'almost all we know'. But we will not and cannot do this, and all we know 'leads men to acknowledge a supreme Being'.[38] In this way it is obvious that God exists.

In addition to this philosophical demonstration of the existence of God, Bolingbroke, having affirmed a law of nature and a mechanical universe, accepted the view that such machinery required a mechanic to start it and this mechanic or demiurge he was willing to call God. The concept of a purely mechanical universe was quite in harmony with many of the scientific notions of his own day, and seemed to derive support from the newtonian theories of gravity and motion. Moreover it had apparent support from the attractive and generally received, but deceptively simple, belief that the world is built on a principle of law. It was inconceivable that the universe and life upon it began without a creator acting in accordance with law. It must be emphasised that, for Bolingbroke, the act of creation was God's only act of revelation, although he appears to believe in a theory of continuous creation.

One of the fundamental principles of the christian message is that the soul is immortal: a belief reinforced by the more specific doctrine of the resurrection of the body. Bolingbroke found that he could not accept the immortality of the soul, or rather, he refused to consider it because his reasoning could not establish its validity. The concept of immortality is a vexatious, puzzling and confounding philosophical problem, not least because the speculative reason alone, when arguing for it, can only establish the *sine qua non*, and when arguing against it can only make an argument *ex silentio*. It may arise from some revelation, now long since forgotten, or from a more simple source, namely, man's inability to believe that with death there is no more, that only a decaying physical object is left. Because the thinking process, the whole life of the mind, is not conditioned by the categories of space and time which it itself employs, because it does not consist simply in sensation and the whole thinking process cannot be observed immediately by sense, it is possible to attribute some immaterial and everlasting qualities to it. In other words, it is possible (in spite of scientific thought that tends to reduce the soul, which is properly speaking a subject, into an impersonal object) to believe in an immortal soul in which something has been created out of nothing. However, this idea is highly ambiguous and confusing unless the materialism implied in some-*thing* and no-*thing* is consciously excluded.

Confronted by this confusion, Bolingbroke rejects the immortality of the soul on the grounds that experience totally disproves it, for as entities cannot be annihilated, they must always exist, although their outward appearance may change. Indivisible particles of matter never change and are by nature eternal: *ex nihilo nihil fit*, and on this basis the immortality of the individually created soul is disproved. Bolingbroke, however, fails to consider creation as more a matter of relationship and composition than of particles which, logically speaking, must be divisible to exist in space, but, if divisible, are not eternal. Moreover he forgets—in pointing to an ultimate indivisibility—that this is the argument by which Plato defends the concept of the immortality of the soul, since bodies only consisting of things made up of component parts are divisible, and thereby destructible, while non-material entities such as the soul are made up of indivisible elements and are, thereby, physically speaking, indestructible and immortal.

To resolve the problem of the soul's creation one can assume that the soul is part of a 'first cause' which will reclaim the soul after death. The soul obviously had a pre-existence, and the 'first cause' is therefore constantly in a process of loss and gain. But from all that is assumed of the 'first cause' this is absurd. Bolingbroke then attempted to resolve the dilemma in which he had placed himself, through trying to combine his non-revelatory materialism with christianity, by denying that the soul was material, but in so doing he did not, of course, resolve any of his difficulties. His solution for the problem is ingenious but hardly profound. He suggests that some matter is given by God the powers of cognition. 'I am persuaded that God can make material systems capable of thought, not only because I must renounce one of the kinds of knowledge that he has given me and the first, though not the principle in the order of knowing, or admit that he has done so; but because the original principles and many of the properties of matter being alike unknown to me, he has not shown to me that it implies any contradiction to assert a material thinking substance.'[39] On this view it would appear to be obvious that there can be no life hereafter, and thus he swept away one of the fundamental precepts of christianity. It can hardly be surprising that his works were received so unfavourably, when he sought to undermine a belief so deeply cherished and so universally held: 'that futurity to which we are all impelled by an inextinguishable thirst for immortality', as Shelley expressed it.

What is God like? Bolingbroke believes in His goodness, which is not prior to, but rather a property of, His wisdom.

> Tho' I think that the moral attributes of the Supreme Being are absorbed, as I expressed myself before, in his wisdom, that we should consider them only as different modifications of this physical attribute, whatever ideas we may frame on the phaenomena, and that we must always talk precariously and impertinently when we presume to apply our ideas of them to the appearances of things; yet I think it proper to shew the divine and the atheist that even the goodness of God is not hard to defend against them both, by everyone who denies, as everyone may most reasonably, the question they beg, and grant in consequence of their alliance to one another.
>
> The wisdom is not discernible by us, as the power of God, nor the goodness as the wisdom. But a multitude of the phaenomena being conformable to our ideas of goodness, we may reason about it . . . If our adversaries shew that men are exposed to many physical and moral evils, we can shew much more good of both kinds that God has bestowed on us, or put it into our power to procure to ourselves. The evils we complain of are constant or occasional effects of the constitution of a world not made for our sakes. But the means to soften some to prevent others, and to palliate and even to cure those that cannot be prevented are so many instances of the positive goodness of God, which ought to be brought to account and set against the evils with greater gratitude and more fairly than they are by men who pass them slightly over, whilst they descend into every particular of the other sort, aggravate the least and declaim pathetically and partially on all.
>
> It would be easy to confirm and illustrate, what is advanced in the physical part of numerous and unanswerable proofs, which are to be found in the writings of natural philosophers. These men have done more service to true theism than all the

metaphysical reasoners *a priori*: or to say something stronger
and equally true, they have done it more service than divines
and atheists in confederacy have done it hurt. It is impossible to read, with attention and without prejudice, what the
former have writ, and not to be convinced by the fact, and
by reason grounded on fact, not on hypothesis, first that we
ought to consider the world we inhabit no otherwise than as a
little wheel in our solar system; nor our solar system any otherwise than as a little but larger wheel in the immense machine
of the universe; and both the one and the other necessary perhaps to the motion of the whole and to the preordained
revolutions in it: nor without being convinced, secondly, that
the wisdom, or, if you had rather say so, the goodness of God
has provided amply for the well-being of man in this world,
and of the whole animal kind, who are objects of the divine
care as well as he, according to their various destinations.[40]

In exalting the wisdom, goodness and power of God Bolingbroke
recognises the perfection of the Deity, but does not presume to say that
this perfection necessarily entails a mechanical theory of rewards and
punishments, salvation and damnation. Justice is no doubt an integral
part of the divine nature, but the precise sphere of its operation is never
indicated by Bolingbroke.

The wisdom of God is reflected in the powers of reason which he
has bestowed on man.

... in man, instinct does no more than point out the first
rudiments of the law of nature. Reason, instructed by experience, shews the law, and the sanctions of it, which are as invari-
able and uniform as the law; for in all ages of the world, and
among all the societies of men, the well-being or the ill-being
of these societies of men, and, therefore, of all mankind has
borne a constant proportion to the observation or neglect of it.
God has given to his human creatures the materials of physical
and moral happiness, if I may so say, in the physical and moral
constitution of things. He has given them faculties, and powers
necessary to collect and apply these materials, and to carry on
the work, of which reason is the architect, as far as these
materials, these faculties, these powers, and the skill of this
architect admit. This the Creator has done for us. What we shall
do for ourselves he has left to the freedom of our elections; for

free-will seems so essential to rational beings, that I presume we cannot conceive any such to be without it, tho' we easily conceive them restrained in the execution of what they will. The plan is that of the divine wisdom; and whatever our imaginations may suggest, we know nothing more particular, and, indeed, nothing at all more of the constitution and order of the human system, nor of the dispensations of providence, than this.[41]

Bolingbroke's religious views may at times have been contradictory, but he was able nevertheless to construct a remarkable system which abandoned all arguments that seemed in any way unreasonable. God was the perfect and omnipotent Being, but He was omnipotent without being omnipresent and, with an olympian aloofness, never indulged in revelation or demonstrated himself particularly. On the other side, man is only an animal endowed with reason whose actions are dominated, not by fears, but by virtue which it is in man's true self-interest to pursue. Man possesses reason and so external authorities are quite superfluous, as with Pope:

> . . . Whatever is, is right;
> That reason, passion, answer one great aim;
> That true self-love and social are the same;
> That virtue only makes our Bliss below;
> And all our Knowledge is, ourselves to know.[42]

In this much of Bolingbroke is summed up. He was a child of his age, and the creed of the eighteenth century was rational behaviour with enlightened self-interest as its driving spirit. This 'true self-love' was as much extolled by Pope and by Bolingbroke as it was damned by Blake who also condemned their natural religion.

> Love seeketh only Self to please,
> To bind another to its delight,
> Joys in another's loss of ease,
> And builds a Hell in Heaven's despite.[43]

It might be said that in Bolingbroke's self-love lay his neglect of party, of country even, and revelational religion. His Hell was a life of loneliness and political exile, a life of rebellion and reflection.

On Society and
Government

Throughout the whole of our history we observe that the leading men who have guided the fortunes of our Commonwealth . . . have invariably agreed in one line of policy—namely to eschew abstractions. This resolution is the distinguishing feature of English statesmanship; it is the principal cause of the duration of the English State; and herein eminently consists the 'wisdom of our ancestors'.

BENJAMIN DISRAELI, *Vindication of the English Constitution*

ONE of the most fundamental concerns of the political theorist is the search for origins. Bolingbroke, however, who was not a professional theorist or philosopher, did not leave a full-scale exposition of his thoughts on this subject. He alludes to the problem in many of his writings, but it is only in his *Fragments of Essays*—numbers X to XVI—that he attempts any serious analysis of the problem. In the *Fragments*, which are highly perceptive, he expresses in brief compass some of his thoughts on the subject. These essays are no more than sketches for a longer study, but in them one can observe the general lines that a more complete study would have taken.

Bolingbroke begins with the premise that man is a social animal, unhappy in isolation, and from this premise he draws the basis of his conclusion: namely, that 'men were never out of society'. Rather it should be said that society existed from the moment when the first man and the first woman joined to produce the first family. After this man progressed from familial or natural to civil society: that is to say, the state in which man's varied needs are most perfectly satisfied. 'Self-sufficiency does not apply to a man living alone, but also to his parents, children and wife, and generally to his friends and fellow-citizens, because man is by nature a social being.'[1]

It is not therefore correct to assume as Hobbes does that while man is not in a political society, society itself does not exist. Each family is its own complete society, and the most natural of societies. There is no compact implied in such a society, unless by some stretch of the imagination the consent of the two parties to live together as man and wife is a form of the lockean contract. It was a natural association. In this, however, Bolingbroke does not exalt the noble savage, nor does he subscribe wholeheartedly to that romantic picture of primitive society which is presented to us by Pope in his *Essay on Man*. 'You poets have given beautiful descriptions of a golden age, with which you suppose the world began. . . . I do not believe that men were as good . . . as you represent them to have been in the primeval world.'[2] Bolingbroke realises that the advance from the natural primeval state is not easy, and that although all men are sociable and it is a natural law for them to be so, such a form of goodness is not irresistible. Man is not always reasonable, and the impulse to form a larger society tends to meet countervailing forces. Mankind does not readily submit to universal rule. In fact the formation of almost any society beyond that of the familial is the result either of overpopulation or, more likely, the fear of conquest or absorption by a more powerful people.

The society which had paternal leadership as its fundamental precept was in fact altered into a civil society by 'mutual conveniency. . . . families or hordes, and the colonies they sent out, unite sometimes for mutual utility with others . . . Reason, which had co-operated with instinct before, takes the place of it now. They coalite amicably by covenants, they make laws by common consent, and from being members of a natural, they become such of a political society.'[3] Authority in the natural society had been represented by the father, while authority in the political society may be represented by the monarch, by an oligarchy or by a legislature. All these impose their laws by common consent, but common consent in the first place does not necessarily mean the contract as it was understood by Locke: that is to say, the formal surrender of individual rights, wholly or in part, to some authority which is above the individual. Rather it signifies an acceptance of the new authority as an extension of the older paternal authority, an authority that had been natural and not artificial, not above the individual but embodying the corporate personality. Thus, man was never purely individual for, while he was in a natural society, though families might be considered to have been individual, men were not, for men were never in such a 'natural' state.

There was, then, a transition from a natural society based on instinct to an 'artificial' society based on reason. Within this transition, however, a continuity must be assumed in outlook and social customs, while there is nevertheless a discontinuity in environment and political composition. And the new societies or unions were in their composition very unlike the old paternal groupings. Paternal society, which might also quite properly be called clan society, implies some form of familial relationship with the head of the society. For this a belief in a common ancestor is sufficient, and indeed the ancestor need not be so by blood but may be an adopted head, and this head of the society has a natural authority over all the constituent members of the familial or clan society. Once, however, this natural authority disappears as a result of the external forces demanding an alteration in the structure and composition of the society, then familial society as such disappears also. The new society held together only by necessity and mutual agreement cannot be assumed to accept the decision of the head of one of its families alone. The new society consisting of several familial groupings would inevitably be larger than the previous group, and the paternal authority of one man cannot by its very nature extend over a vast number if the membership of the group has no clan relationship. In this case, Bolingbroke declares, it becomes 'necessary to establish a power superior to that of the fathers of families, and, as fast as men went out of a state of nature, to substitute artificial to natural government'.[4] Monarchy is the logical development of natural government, and as natural government was designed for the good of the people, so also is civil government of which monarchy is the name given to one form of that manifestation.

Having established 'artificial' government, Bolingbroke considers that logically it must have been monarchy, because after the troublesome formative period of the new societies, after the oligarchic factions, the monarch would always emerge as the 'father of his people', who embodied their will and was organically one with them, e.g. Seneca's

De Clementia: *Tu* [Nero] *animus rei publicae tuae es, illa corpus tuum.*[5]
Bolingbroke takes issue with those who think that the new governments would have been democracies. He reasons in the following
manner: the fathers, having once had power, would not care to share
it with all men and would promote an aristocratic or oligarchic regime;
the people would not then have tolerated oligarchy and would
logically have supported monarchy. Monarchy would in its first form
have been not too dissimilar to the familial traditions which had been
the common experience. Aristocracy and democracy would both be
new forms and, because of their newness, not entirely congenial to the
ordinary mind. Certainly, in spite of Bolingbroke's unflattering
appraisal of Filmer's paternal king thesis, there could be no doubt that
this paternal king was much more traditional than any concept of
egalitarian democracy. No family is democratic and it was only the
familial experience—that is to say the natural government which had
existed earlier—on which men could draw for their constitutional
ideas.

The royal power was limited; Bolingbroke always assumed that
the best monarchies were those where the sovereign did not have
unlimited power. The idea of totalitarianism, the absolutism of a
deified state, was unknown to him, and in *The Idea of a Patriot King* his
ideal ruler is portrayed as the monarch who is above party, governing
according to the constitution. The custom or law of a family society
existed, and from this collection of customs derived the traditions
governing the action of the king. Custom may in a sense be equated
with justice, and may then become the new constitution. The 'first
kings had neither arbitrary nor legislative power by virtue of any real
prerogative; on the contrary, they were chosen kings because they were
chosen legislators, and the goodness of the laws recommended them to
the throne and maintained them on it'.[6] Law-making was not necessarily the function of the monarchy, but, because of the requirements of
the law, society became monarchical. The kings were chosen and given
the sovereignty by the people, but they were always accountable for
the use they made of their authority. 'For we must all appear before
the judgment seat of Christ.'[7]

Bolingbroke here reflects the concept of the 'godly prince' of the
Reformers and the democratic kingship of the Old Testament, and rejects
an arbitrary caesaro-papism. Kingship is instituted by consent or by the
law of nature and has, like all other institutions which conform to the law
of nature, divine approbation. Sovereignty, once the prized possession

of the patriarch, is now vested in the king and the latter's authority is binding on all people. Bolingbroke denies the ideas of Filmer that Adam 'was an absolute monarch by creation; that his right descended to kings; that all other men are slaves by birth and never had a right to choose either forms of government or governors'.[8] By this argument either all men are kings because they are the sons of Adam, or else none are except some special heirs, and these have yet to be found. For to assume that men who are sovereigns inevitably are the true heirs of Adam, while those who are subjects are not, is an absurdity. Royal authority and power have been acquired by so many devious methods, royal descent being but one, that to designate kings alone as the sons of Adam is to deny most of the facts of history. Either Adam was the first man and we are all his descendants, since it is after all generally assumed that man inherited his sin, or Adam was the progenitor of a special line of kings and the rest of mankind descends from some other line, in which case kings are the sinners par excellence. It is however generally accepted, as a convenient hypothesis, that Adam was the first man and that from him come all men, and one simply cannot have it both ways.

Bolingbroke refuses to accept the idea that, if men may create governments or even choose the sovereign, they cannot at the same time grant such a thing as sovereignty. It has been claimed that sovereignty can only come from God. But this is, in Bolingbroke's eyes, ridiculous. Monarchy is 'like every other form of government . . . [a] human institution, established by the people, and for the people, and . . . no other majesty, since that word imposes so much, is inherent in it than that which belongs to the supreme power of every state, wherever that power is placed'.[9] The implication is that man cannot create something more sovereign than himself. Individually and by himself he may not be able to do so, but then he was never in a position to do so. The group, however, or the family, which allows one of its members to be more sovereign than any of its individual component parts, can confer its authority on someone external. He thus has more sovereignty than the members of the group, and if several familial groups bestow their sovereignty on one man they have created one who is more sovereign than each of the groups separately. Thus the king comes to represent a combined sovereignty, and no external authority for determining this is necessary. He is therefore constituted sovereign and is not constitutive of sovereignty.

But a king, once chosen, is the king: he has the royal prerogatives and majesty automatically in *connubium felice*. Bolingbroke thus tempers democracy with the rigidity of a congé d'élire. An analogy might be found in the religious world of Tibet. When the Dalai Lama is reincarnated and the Tibetans discover the child whose body his spirit has chosen to inhabit, the child is immediately recognised as the Dalai Lama. He is not, however, elected as such. The acts of homage, coronation and enthronement—all made with divine approbation and under the divine ægis—are merely the external sacraments of an already accomplished fact. There cannot be that strange misunderstanding which seems to persist in the minds of many, that a king is not a king until he has received some similar affirmations of his status, for to the Tibetan the act of reincarnation accomplishes everything and the Dalai Lama is the Dalai Lama.

Civil government originated, then, from nature; not by the agreement of separate individuals each divesting themselves of an inherent sovereignty, but by the coalescence of family groups. Bolingbroke here gives expression to what might be designated the 'compact theory' of the origin of government. His ideas are not unlike those of the advocates of the thesis that the federal government in the United States was created by the states and not by the people. Bolingbroke is very firm in his insistence on this point, if only to deny the general precepts of Hooker on the original nature of man. He parts company, too, with Locke in holding that the latter's view of the law of nature, which allowed each man to 'exercise justice for himself... on those who violated this law',[10] was based on false premises. Locke had argued: 'If we may not suppose men ever to have been in the state of nature because we hear not much of them in such a state, we may as well suppose the armies of Solmanasser or Xerxes were never children, because we hear little of them till they were men, and embodied in armies.'[11] Bolingbroke will have none of this. Of course these men were children; anyone who supposes to the contrary would be a lunatic, and in fact there are few persons in any mythology who spring fully armed from the head of Zeus. The real difficulty is in the definition of 'state of nature'; the question is whether it was composed of men living in family groups who joined together to form civil government, or whether it was 'composed of as many solitary individuals as there were men in the world, and whether these men, independent and equal one amongst another, met amicably together, and set up a government without any better preparation for it'.[12] Put in these terms, and with a true regard for the nature of man, the whole idea is ludicrous. The image of independent, equal sovereigns creating civil authority is as romantic as the notion of Lucretius that all his independent and equally moving atoms could by a slight swerve create an ordered universe.

Bolingbroke also questions the whole concept of equality, which he classifies as personal and social. Personal equality he regards simply as an illusion. He declares (without, however, giving any proof of this) that 'the creatures of no other species are probably so unequal in this respect as those of the human'.[13] Presumably he means that the endowments given to man are not the same in every case; some men as a result of heredity are naturally intelligent, others naturally stupid and no amount of education and environmental influence will really change the case. Social equality, on the other hand, does exist in that all men are subject to authority, and can be regarded as equal in the eyes of the law. He accepts a partial egalitarianism here, but that is all.

On the state of man himself, Bolingbroke accepts the premise that all are born free, but that then comes the decision as to whether they are to continue so or to become servile. Freedom consists essentially in the freedom of choice between the traditional alternatives of being the one who obeys orders, or the one who gives them. Bolingbroke uses this notion of freedom to attack the lockean conception of the state of nature. He declares that the real state of perfect freedom would have been the hobbesian state: 'a state of war and violence, of mutual and alternate oppression'.[14] Locke, however, postulates a situation in which there was a law of nature which was to limit the violence, but each man as a result of the equality principle was to be the sole arbiter of the law. In such a situation each man could not fail to see events entirely in his own interest and the result would be anarchy; the state of freedom which might exist in theory for each man would in fact be so limited by the actions of others that it would be meaningless.

Bolingbroke thus exposes the specious identification of freedom with independence, and will not accept any of the extensions of Locke's natural law. Locke had questioned whether a state may punish a man who owes no allegiance to the state, but in answering affirmatively had based his answer on his libertine law of nature. Bolingbroke takes quite a different view. An alien is protected by the state even though he is not a subject of it; he has accepted its protection and thus its authority and can therefore very logically be punished if he violates that authority. He is punished, not by the law of nature, but by virtue of his own consent. The individual, being free to choose, has relinquished *ab initio* the quest of a mythical independence, and has accepted the obligations of his organic relationship with the rest of mankind. This is very significant in that he is then punished by the community or state as a whole, and not by some one individual acting as a private arbiter of a 'law of nature'. The people in their collective state are not merely acting from the individual viewpoint; their rights and powers are of a different nature.

Bolingbroke, while differing sharply with Locke, does not impugn his motives. He does consider, however, that Locke was extreme in many of his ideas and decidedly unhistorical. If man had lived in a state of naturalness as Locke would have us suppose then man would not have survived. A collective family existence is the natural state of society and man was always part of such a society. Assuming that each family gave its consent to union and did so after a unanimous vote, this would imply man was part of some communal arrangement before he joined Locke's civil society. The lockean state of nature, in fact, never existed, and even supposing that it was postulated in order to guarantee man's natural rights, it could only serve 'to give us a notion of natural liberty very different from the real constitution of nature'.[15] Civilisation, then, did not arise through free men 'joining' society, as people join a club.

Neither is it logical to assume that men joined society—that is to say civil society, for they were already in natural society—for any other reason than their own welfare. Enlightened self-interest is for Bolingbroke a more active catalyst than all the high-sounding dogmas of collective equality. Utility, not idealism, promoted government. There may be a law of nature which appeals to all men—indeed Bolingbroke thinks there is—but this law of nature is a matter of reason, and reason does not always predominate. Emotion plays a vast rôle in man's life, and man is fallible, frequently inexperienced. Civil society is indeed far from perfect, but its origins were good, and if natural law, properly understood, can be applied to society in such a way that its rationale circumscribes our diverse human emotions, then 'the state in which man's varied needs are most perfectly satisfied'[16] can function as it should.

Having reviewed Bolingbroke's general theories on government, we must now turn to consider what he does with practical cases. In particular we will consider his analysis of the British constitution which appears in the series of essays entitled *A Dissertation Upon Parties*. In these essays, which are a mixture of constitutional theory, history and polemic, Bolingbroke manages to convey his conception of the framework of the British constitution. He admits freely that prior to 1688 there were two basic theories of the constitution, but since that time only one can be properly said to exist. He declares: 'Our constitution is no longer a mystery; the power of the crown is now exactly limited, the chimera or prerogative removed and the rights of the subject are no longer problematical.'[17] It is this demythologised constitution which he intends to illumine in various aspects. We must first, however, be clear precisely what Bolingbroke understood by the word 'constitution'.

> By constitution we mean, whenever we speak with propriety and exactness, that assemblage of laws, institutions and customs, derived from certain fixed principles of reason, directed to certain fixed objects of public good, that compose the general system, according to which the community hath agreed to be governed. By government we mean, whenever we speak in the same manner, that particular tenor of conduct which a chief magistrate, or inferior magistrates under his direction and influence, hold in the administration of public affairs.[18]

His avowed intention is not to discuss civil government, as such, but his essays are in a very real sense discussions of a particular government and its failures. His purpose in writing these essays was to attack the government of King George II by attacking the administration of Robert Walpole. Nevertheless, it is possible, and indeed perfectly feasible, to disregard for the moment the motives underlying his constitutional writings.

In his *Idea of a Patriot King* Bolingbroke wrote that he thought 'a limited monarchy the best of governments . . . and . . . an hereditary monarchy the best of monarchies'.[19] As regards the problem of hereditary monarchy, one finds him placing curbs on this statement. He accepts the hereditary principle, but does not do so blindly, for this can lead to a reversal of the concept of 'limited monarchy' which he supports.

> If a divine, indefeasible, hereditary right . . . be once acknowledged: a right independent of the community, and which vests in every successive prince immediately on the death of his predecessor, and previously to any engagement taken on his part

towards the people; if the people once acknowledge themselves bound to such princes by the ties of passive obedience and non-resistance, by an allegiance unconditional and not reciprocal to protection; [then a sovereign has] the power, if not the right, given [him of tyranny and] princes who have the power, are prone to think that they have the right.[20]

The monarchs of England, however, have never had such power that they could enforce this 'right', and they have always been accepted on other terms than those of simple hereditary right. Kings must receive the acclamation of society through its representatives. Bolingbroke insists that from Saxon times onwards the new king had to be recognised by parliament or something very much like it. To assume that parliament did not so act is to ignore the plain facts of history; one need only note the accessions of Henry IV and Henry VII to see the truth of this statement. It is, we may note, in accord with his general theory of origins, in which he presents a rational account of the appointment of the first king, who received his powers from society and at their consent.

Since the Revolution of 1688 the rôle of the king has been defined with a greater degree of clarity.

A king of Britain is now, strictly and properly, what kings should always be, a member, but the supreme member, or the head of a political body: part of one individual specific whole, in every respect, distinct from it or independent of it in none: he can no longer move in another orbit from his people, and, like some superior planet, attract, repel, influence, and direct their motions by his own. He and they are parts of the same system, intimately joined and co-operating together, acting and acted upon, limiting and limited, controlling and controlled by one another; and when he ceases to stand in this relation to them, he ceases to stand in any. The settlements, by which he governs, are plainly original contracts. His institution is plainly conditional, and he may forfeit his right to allegiance, as undeniably and effectually, as the subject may forfeit his right to protection. There are no longer any hidden reserves of authority, to be let out on occasion, and to overflow the rights and privileges of the people. The laws of the land are known, and they are the sole springs from whence the prince can derive his pretensions, and the people theirs.[21]

Arising from this strictly orthodox definition of the constitutional monarch, a number of points are to be noted. The king is no longer a priestly figure; he is the chief magistrate of a political society. He is no longer the romantic patriarchal figure—the father-image postulated by Filmer. The king is not conterminous with the state; neither is he outside the whole process of government. He cannot act outside the system as a *solus* entity, and is indeed but one part of a political organism that has at least two parts. These are mutually dependent; neither can act to govern society without the other, and neither is totally supreme. The sovereign is not outside the law and he cannot claim extra-legal authority for his acts. The body of the common law, mediated by preceding generations, is something that is 'given' to the people as a whole, something that is objective and not to be changed by one man's whim. For the king, therefore, to claim such things as the dispensing power is to violate the relationship established since the Revolution.

The most significant point, perhaps, of this conception of law is that the king is thus involved in a contractual relationship with his people. In his general theory Bolingbroke has specifically denied that a contract as such exists at all or indeed ever did. Yet here he is, in fact, proceeding well in the lockean tradition to propound what logically follows this concept of contract (and which also he has denied earlier): namely, that if the contract be violated by the sovereign the people may rebel. He does not, however, venture to sanction openly a call to arms, but contents himself with saying that 'if grievances should grow intolerable . . . if redress should become absolutely desperate; if liberty itself should be in imminent peril; the nature of our constitution would justify . . . resistance' to the tyrant.[22]

The king is a trustee for the sovereignty of the people. Moreover, he only exists as an embodiment of that sovereignty which is not the personal property of the people but which is, however, a real estate of which they hold the title deeds. Consequently he does not own them or their property or their taxes personally. He may have a life interest in some part of their wealth, and indeed he does this through the civil list which is voted to him, but the whole of the national revenue is not his to call upon at will. He does not even own all of the public revenue, and although he may have the direction of it, parliament designates the expenditure. The sovereign is here limited very specifically, and the old concept of the national treasury and the royal pocket, as being one and the same for all occasions, is disallowed. The control of finance is one of parliament's chief weapons for maintaining the balance between monarch and people.

The king is 'part of one individual specific whole', the head of the body politic. The king exercises the executive power, but 'the legislative, or supreme power, is vested . . . in three estates, whereof the king is one, whilst the members of the other two preserve their private independency, except that which is in the scheme of our constitution.'[23] Lawmaking requires that all three estates should operate together in a harmonious fashion, with each functioning independently of the others and yet being dependent on them in the making of law. No single estate can make law, neither can any two of them. This latter statement is perhaps open to some qualification in that laws were passed by the Convention to settle the crown on William and Mary, but this was a special procedure employed to meet special circumstances. The legislative bodies require the fiat of the sovereign but must, in order to function properly, exist collaterally with him.

These separate estates are, of course, the Lords and Commons. The latter is simply taken as representing the freemen of society. In all of these essays Bolingbroke makes no particular mention of the franchise; he seems to operate on the general assumption that this is so widely understood as to need no elaboration. It would seem, too, that he assumes that all free men are represented in the Commons and that is all that is necessary. It is a body which, in order to function properly, must be elected with a relative frequency—according to Bolingbroke about every three years—because in this fashion 'the people [can] . . . secure their interests . . . by mending their choice of trustees'.[24] To maintain its independence the elections must be free and unhampered. Not only must the Crown remain outside the electoral arena, but it must ensure that its minions do likewise; equally the Lords must stand aside from electoral conflict.

The third segment of the legislative power between the sovereign and the commonalty is the aristocracy. This group, represented by the peerage, might not seem to be a check on the Crown and a balance in the constitution, since peers are created by the Crown, and so it would appear they are subservient to it. This, however, would only be the case if peers were created *ad libitum*, which does not happen. It did, of course, occur when twelve peers were created in a batch in order to ensure the ratification of the Treaty of Utrecht. Bolingbroke implies that this mass use of the prerogative met 'with universal and most just disapprobation'.[25] As this is quite contrary to the way he felt when he was in office advising Queen Anne to use her prerogative, it hardly shows him in a very favourable light. Such lapses are not perhaps unexpected in a politician, but they do cast doubt on the honesty of his other views.

A peer's rights can 'never' be removed; 'never' is perhaps an over-statement and 'hardly ever' should be substituted, for a peer may lose his rights by forfeiture, as Bolingbroke himself had done. Since the peerage is small in number, ancient and independent, all peers can sit as by inherent right. 'The peers are . . . accountable for their conduct . . . to God, to their own consciences, to the tribunal of public fame, and to no other.'[26] They make up a body which Bolingbroke sees as depending 'neither on the king nor the people', and 'they constitute a middle order, and are properly mediators between the other two, in the eye of . . . the constitution'.[27]

The British constitution, like the Roman constitution as inter-preted by Polybius, is a mixture of 'monarchical, aristocratical and democratical power',[28] and because of this system of mixed elements, each counterbalancing the others, freedom is maintained. Violation of the principles embodied in such a system, whichever of the groups were responsible, has led 'to salutary revolutions'.[29] When the fear of revolu-tion has passed it is then safe to refer to past revolutions as salutary, but whether future ones may be so designated is not always so obvious. For the moment a state of balance obtains and harmony is preserved. Parliament has reduced royal authority and kept it in bounds, while the sovereign has contained parliament's enthusiasms and excesses by his prerogative. The dynamic equilibrium of a mixed government has all of the virtues, and alternatives have little to recommend them. Arbitrary governments

> stand in direct opposition to the sole motive of submission to any government whatsoever; for if men quit the state, and renounce the rights of nature, . . . they do this, that they may not remain exposed to the arbitrary will of other men, the weakest to that of the strongest, the few to that of the many. Now . . . for fear of being exposed to arbitrary will sometimes, they choose to be governed by it always. These governments . . . are tyranny in their very institutions; and they who submit to them are slaves.[30]

The autocracy of France is alien to the grey skies of the English compromise between rulers and ruled. Complete democracy on the other hand, which is often a reaction against sheer autocracy, seems to many so reasonable 'because here it is the will of the whole community that governs the whole community'.[31] But it is a logical impossibility for the whole to govern the whole, and in practice it disregards minority rights, is deluded by its own desires, and is subject to every fickle wind of unreasonableness. The result is not only tyranny—differing, it is true, from the tyranny of the arbitrary individual will—but also anarchy, which Bolingbroke, as a good son of the Augustan age, deplores. Oligarchy, which is a hybrid constitution, he considers equally dangerous for 'if the few who govern are united', then tyranny of a very violent nature frequently follows, while 'if they are disunited' they dissolve 'into factions and disorders as great as those of the most tumultuous democracy'.[32]

It must be observed that his mixed government, the several parts of which are mutually dependent, is not the imaginary government of Montesquieu who thought there should be a separation of elements; namely, the executive, legislative and judicial. Nowhere in Bolingbroke's writings is this said or even implied. Government consists of various entities, but to make government they are one. It does not consist of separate entities in themselves, but of separate entities forming one whole. (Rather like three Persons of one Triune God.)

As has been noted, in his account of the Commons he says nothing about franchise, but on other aspects of parliament he is more explicit. He believes in annual sessions and in strict parliamentary control of finance. He thinks that parliament should be elected frequently, so that

> the representatives should have frequent opportunities to communicate together about national grievances; to complain of them, and to obtain redress of them, in an orderly, solemn, legal manner; and that the people should have frequent opportunities of calling their representatives to account, as it were for the discharge of the trust committed to them, and of approving or disapproving their conduct by electing or not electing them anew.[33]

He considers in the first place

> that nothing could make it safe, nor therefore reasonable to repose in any sort of men whatsoever, so great a trust as the collective body of delegates to the representatives in this

> kingdom except the shortness of the term for which the trust is delegated. Secondly that every prolongation of this term is, therefore, in its degree, unsafe for the people; that it weakens their security, and endangers liberty by the very powers given for its preservation. Thirdly that such prolongations expose the nation, in the possible case of having a corrupt parliament, to lose the great advantage which our constitution hath provided of curing the evil, before it grows conformed and desperate, by the gentle method, of choosing a new representative, and reduce the nation, by consequence, to have no other alternative than that of submitting or resisting; though submission will be as grievous; and resistance much more difficult when the legislature betrays its trust, than when the king abuses his power.[34]

While frequent elections may be inconvenient to some and a curb on government efficiency, they prevent the continued power of an oligarchy and permit the lamp of national liberty to burn with fresh life.

The 'constitution is not . . . a jumble of disjointed, incoherent whimsies, but a noble and wise system, the essential parts of which are so proportioned, and so intimately connected, that a change in one begets a change in the whole'.[35] Balance is his watchword. He does not see imbalance arising from royal concessions to parliament, or from the Lords to the Commons, but rather from parliament's giving way to the sovereign. 'A king cannot be tempted to give up the interest of the crown, because he cannot give up this public interest without giving up his private interest; whereas the members of such assemblies may promote their private interest, by sacrificing to it that of the public.'[36] At the same time the nobility can gain nothing from permitting the liberty of the Commons to be removed, for the Crown alone is the gainer. Initially, of course, the Lords might not regard the destruction of popular liberty as the first violation of the contract, but if the latter is violated in one direction this could be the thin end of the wedge, and so in due course the nobility would lose their rights as well. To preserve the balance of the constitution it is absolutely essential that all parts function in their respective spheres or else tyranny of some sort or another will result; as Alcmæon declared: 'The bond of health is the "equal balance" of the powers.'

The constitution is an organic whole, and is in itself immutable. Even if an opportunity arose to alter the constitution, men would choose this constitution. Although in each minute form and detail it is not always the same, in essence it remains unaltered. Even as far back as the time of the Saxons there were assemblies which were the direct progenitors of parliament; and democratic rights have, in spite of numerous attempts at usurpation, never been surrendered. Even the monarchy, which may have lost some of its superfluous privileges but none of its essential rights, is really the same.

> A popular king of Great Britain will be always not only secure but in effect absolute. He will be, what the British constitution alone can make any prince, the absolute monarch of a free people; and this popularity is so easily acquired, a king gains the public confidence and affection at so cheap a rate that he must be very poor indeed in all the kingly virtues, who does not purchase them, and establish true popularity upon them.[37]

We can see, then, how the Commons' power is not such as to be able *solus* to overthrow the Crown and the Lords. The Commons, however, in alliance with one or both is able to overbalance the constitution, and when standing alone can rebuff the other two. The Lords possess an intermediate status; they are, as it were, the helmsmen for the captain and crew of the ship of state. But when the constitution is right there are no contentions between parts, for all have the proper aim of government. 'To govern a society by a constitution founded on the eternal rules of right reason, and directed to promote the happiness of the whole, and of every individual, is the noblest prerogative which can belong to humanity; and if man may be said, without profaneness to imitate God in any case, this is the case.'[38]

Bolingbroke does not support the view that parliament and sovereign together are absolutely supreme. They are not permitted to annul the constitution. If this were to occur, the initial contract would be broken, for not only do prince and people have an agreement, but there is also an agreement between the people and their representative assemblies. In such a case, therefore, the people would be no longer bound to obey. 'The collective body of the people of Great Britain delegate but do not give up; trust, but do not alienate their right and power.' The people would either restore the lost constitution or create a new one. The right of revolution is always retained in the last resort.

A blatant usurpation through annulment of the constitution is very unlikely, for there are other more effective ways of doing much the same thing while still giving lip-service to the outward form of the constitution. Bolingbroke admonishes society to be especially watchful of those who appear to be the friends of the constitution but in reality are the enemies of it. Such men will promote standing armies; they will create alarms to frighten the people out of their liberties; and they will deliberately corrupt society, thus making it less concerned for its freedoms. Such men will overburden the public with taxes on the specious reasoning that the money is necessary for the national welfare, while their intention is that it should be used to undermine public morale. Frugality will be destroyed, and frugality, as Bolingbroke sees with the hindsight of the rake rather than the vision of the prophet, is an outstanding sign of character which, once lost, is almost impossible to recover. The sumptuary laws of a Sulla may be of little avail, but to safeguard the constitution excessive affluence and luxury must be prevented.

In fine, Bolingbroke sees the British constitution as a 'system of government suited to the genius of our nation, and even to our situation. The experience of many hundreds of years hath shown, that by preserving this constitution inviolate, or by drawing back to the principles on which it was originally founded, whenever it shall be made to swerve from them, we may secure to ourselves and to our latest posterity the possession of that liberty which we have long enjoyed.'[40]

On Political Parties

Bolingbroke, so long as he was a practising statesman, was a strict party man, indeed much too violent as a party man, carrying his partisanship further than his wiser colleague, Oxford, wished; it was only as a philosopher out of office that Bolingbroke found the party groups sour and advised the abolition of the party system by a 'patriot King.' . . . The evils which Bolingbroke denounced under the first two Georges . . . were real evils, but they were the result not of the two-party system, but, on the contrary, of its partial abeyance. Under George I and II the Tory party was too weak to be an effective opposition . . . England was being governed not on the two-party system but by a single party . . . with no rivals to criticise or check their greed.

> G. M. TREVELYAN: *The Two Party System in English Political History*

EVEN as Bolingbroke was writing his most severe and scurrilous attacks on his political opponents, he was presenting ideas which were to have a larger significance. In his *Dissertation Upon Parties*—nominally a plea for good government, but actually a call for the overthrow of his hated rival Walpole—he gives one of the earliest accounts of the history of political parties. The idea of such a history was perhaps taken from Davenant or more directly from Rapin's *Dissertation sur les Whigs et les Tories*, but it is distinctive in being one of the clearest accounts of party government written by a contemporary and a participant. Of all of the subjects written on by Bolingbroke, this is the one where his own personal knowledge and insight were greatest. It is clear that a good deal in his other historical writing is suspect, based as it is on the technique of *suppressio veri*, *suggestio falsi* for the purposes of his own particular thesis. But in this case his writing has more merit than that possessed by mere polemic.

That Bolingbroke is opposed to 'political party' must be taken as axiomatic; he assumes that party is faction and that faction blocks the whole process of government. He assumes also that his opponents are factional (for the moment at least he himself is out of office and power). He therefore acts as the spokesman for the 'country party', and claims that this party is the *only* party which can be considered to be the true spokesman for the national interest.

The definitions which he propounds for basic party beliefs have been traditionally accepted, and many generalising historians would feel no hesitation in using them as good working definitions. The precepts of the whigs, for example, consisted in 'the power and majesty of the people, an original contract, the authority and independency of parliament, liberty, resistance, exclusion, abdication, and deposition'.[1] Tory principles were: 'divine hereditary, indefeasible right, lineal succession, passive obedience, prerogative, non-resistance, . . . nay, and sometimes popery too'.[2] These canons of political belief which Bolingbroke enumerates were generally true and generally applicable. Yet to suppose that each side rejected all of the precepts of the other entailed a concept of a two-party system which was very much of an over-simplification, as modern historians realise. The tories were never so agreed as to the precepts ascribed to them as Bolingbroke would have it believed, and in fact one might well say that the tories were more factional than their whig opponents. Moreover, a certain number of their old beliefs were discarded at the time of the Revolution of 1688, when most Englishmen, whether whig or tory, were 'really united; united on principles of liberty'.[3] The political conflicts of the day were not about Jacobites and republicans, or even matters of policy, but were about who should govern the country.

Before explaining the rise of party, Bolingbroke shows the truth of the view that men were united on principles of liberty and continued to be so united, by pointing out the growing toleration afforded to dissenters and the general acceptance of them by Anglicans. The other indication of unity was the common acceptance of the Revolution of 1688. It was a reformatory event for it had established 'new interests, new principles of government, new measures of submission, and new obligations'.[4] The royal succession was derived from it, as were more explicit statements of ancient privileges. On such a basis 'all the reason-able whigs and tories unite'.[5] The whigs 'have always professed the principles which paved the way for the revolution; and whatever the tories may have professed, they acted upon the same principles, or they acted upon none, . . . when they brought about the great event, [the deposition of James II] in concert with the rest of the nation'.[6] Granting the existence of this halcyon situation in 1688–9, how can it be that a storm should have arisen to destroy it? This has happened, Bolingbroke argues, because men have not remained united, they have lost their principles through corruption and have assisted in the rise of faction, and of them 'who nourish and propagate it, who eat themselves, and tempt others to eat the baneful fruit it bears'.[7]

Parties have not always dominated the English political stage. Queen Elizabeth had the majority of her people in support of her; she led a united society: a society such as Bolingbroke wished to see restored. For his history it was essential to maintain the general truth of this thesis, and he pursued with vigour the utopian image of a united society. On Elizabeth, as we have seen (pages 65–66), he bestows a panegyric, repeated in *The Idea of a Patriot King* (page 137 below), finding in her reign that golden age which should be a model for his own and later ages. He recognises that she engaged in certain political manoeuvres, but claims that fundamentally there were no parties as such. This is, of course, only partially true, and even Bolingbroke admits that differences of opinion existed. 'Opinions very different from those which received the sanction of a legal establishment in church and state had crept about obscurely if not silently, even whilst the government of Elizabeth lasted.'[8]

The golden age, in fact, soon began to vanish, and its united society disintegrated under the extravagant notions of prerogative government held by her immediate successors. The result was that 'all the fury of faction and enthusiasm was employed to destroy the constitution to the very foundations'.[9] The civil war created two groups and the united national society was shattered almost beyond repair. The restoration, however, seemed to achieve—if only temporarily—the unification of society, the result of the good sane views of Clarendon: a great statesman and spokesman of the national interest. On this occasion 'Great lenity was shown . . . this conduct would have gone far towards restoring the nation to its primitive temper and integrity, to its old good manners, its old good humour, and its old good nature';[10] but unfortunately this spirit was not maintained.

Parties were gradually re-formed, and they bore 'unhappily too near a resemblance to the constitution of parties before the [civil] war'.[11] Fears of republicanism and the distresses of the Cromwellian interlude bred a 'high flying' authoritarian temper in many supporters of the restored monarchy.

> Hereditary, indefeasible right, passive obedience and non-resistance, those cornerstones, which are an improper foundation for any superstructure but that of tyranny, were made, even by parliament, the foundation of the monarchy; and all those, who declined an exact and strict conformity to the whole establishment of the church, even to the most minute parts of it, were deprived of the protection, nay exposed to the prosecution of the state. . . . Roundhead and cavalier were, in effect, no more. Whig and tory were not yet in being. The only two apparent parties were those of churchmen and dissenters; and religious differences alone at this time maintained the distinction.[12]

Parties arose, according to Bolingbroke, because of clerical enthusiasm; and he finds it impossible to disguise his anticlerical spirit. It is over-stating matters, however, to say that religious factionalism was the sole parent of the new party system. The loss of principles through corruption had resulted in a power-disintegration of which the *odium theologicum* was the symptom and not the cause. Religious differences were none the less very much involved in the line of development, since they constituted a natural medium of expression for those who sought to direct temporal affairs.

If religious differences divided men into camps which could evolve into parties, what actually promoted the creation of organised parties? According to Bolingbroke the spirit of partisanship was heightened by the effects of a new dualism: the court and the national interest. As long as court and national interest were indistinguishable—as they had been in the Tudor period or at the time of the Restoration—the state of relative unity continued; but with the death of Southampton and the dismissal of Clarendon a new situation resulted. 'It is sufficient . . . to observe, that the tide of party which had run so strongly for the court, and had been seldom so much as slackened hitherto, began now to turn, to run year after year more strongly the other way.'[13] Even the pensioners and placemen began to show signs of increasing independence. But because the court was poor it could not corrupt parliament, and so the nation did not yet become embroiled in what might be termed party politics. Indeed, there was as yet no absolute division of interests between the Crown and the nation, or between one segment of society and another. Not yet had a political sectionalism sapped the idea of national unity. Yet gradually and inexorably during Charles II's reign this dichotomy of interests developed.

The 'moment of truth', the emergence of an inward factional corruption, came with the Popish Plot and the Exclusion Bill. The latter, instead of being 'carried on in the spirit of a country party' and supported 'with a national concurrence',[14] became the tool of a faction; while the former invoked the spirit of faction to secure its aims. Charles II, who hitherto had usually acquiesced in the more extreme demands of parliament, now resisted. The extremism of the exclusionists, combined with the obstinate resistance of the king, provided the 'opportunity of breaking the country party, of dividing the nation into whig and tory'.[15] Thus the real creators of political parties were the king himself and those wild men who wished absolutely to prohibit James from the succession. As a result of their action the old national union disintegrated.

Bolingbroke considered that

> [the] country party must be authorized by the voice of the country. It must be formed on principles of common interest. It cannot be united and maintained on particular prejudices, any more than it can, or ought to be, directed to the particular interests of any set of men whatsoever. A party, thus constituted, is improperly called party. It is the nation speaking and acting in the discourse and conduct of particular men.[16]

Bolingbroke in his idealism identifies this national country party with that unity of society which had disintegrated under the pressure of events. The immediate consequence of this disintegration was that each individual began to follow his own private inclinations, and to support those whom he disapproved of the least. In this explosive situation

> Whig and tory were now formed into parties; ... The whigs were not roundheads ... The tories were not cavaliers ... The whigs were not dis enters nor republicans, though they favoured the former, and though some inconsiderable remains of the latter might find shelter in their party. The tories had no disposition to become slaves, or papists, though they abetted the

exercise of an exorbitant power by the crown, and though they supported the pretensions of a popish successor to it.[17]

Once the parties were organised, their separation was supported 'by mutual jealousies and fears, which are often sufficient to nourish themselves, when they have once taken root in the mind, and which were at this time watered and cultivated with all the factious industry possible'.[18] Party hostility was maintained in the tradition of the Guelf and Ghibelline controversies of the middle ages; 'prerogative, not money'[19] was used to sustain the conflict. The parties, however, were not such as to be hardened permanently and rigidly; 'the spirit of liberty remained in many, uncorrupted and unextinguished'.[20]

Although Charles II, in Bolingbroke's view, had been one of the progenitors of party, he was not purely a party sovereign. He attempted as far as possible to be king of a united people. 'He observed their temper, and he complied with it. . . . King Charles was too wise to push the nation to an . . . extremity.'[21] Even so, at the conclusion of his reign faction prevailed. Frenzy and violence continued unabated, jealousies and prejudices were unassuaged. This was the situation at the accession of James II, and the whole of his reign was one long factional conflict.

England, however, was fortunate even in its disasters, and the two factions suddenly saw reason. They 'had sacrificed their country to their party', but now, as though purged by their excesses and madnesses, they sacrificed 'their party to their country'.[22] External pressure had once more created internal unity. The extreme assumptions of James united all factions, for all were agreed that the continued rule of such a king was impossible. The national interest—that dormant country party, Bolingbroke's *Britannia rediviva*—awoke and once more dominated the scene. The sacrifice of party purified the nation. 'The revolution was a fire, which purged off the dross of both parties; and the dross being purged off, they appeared to be of the same metal, and answered the same standard.'[23]

A situation arose not unlike that of 1660, and during the crisis moderation and good sense prevailed. The new government was not based on the exclusive platform of either party. Extremists attempted to undo the work of union but they were not successful, save in that they did furnish 'pretence to factions, who kept up a division under the old names, when the differences were really extinguished by the conduct of both parties, because the conduct of both parties was no longer conformable to the principles imputed to them'.[24] Neither party, in fact, was willing to answer to the preconceived notions of extremist politicians. By the settlement of 1688 the whigs had shown they were not republicans, for the monarchy still existed and so did the established Anglican church; while the tories had likewise demonstrated that they were not in favour of prerogative government or of religious bigotry.

Nevertheless when the fire of crisis had burnt itself out, the old party structures could be rebuilt, albeit of different materials. 'The real essences of whig and tory were ... destroyed, but the nominal were preserved, and have done since that time a good part of the mischief which the real did before.'[25] Private desires and personal hopes did much to recreate the spirit of faction, and, once the excitement was over, former prejudices reappeared, old animosities were revived. Even though events had demonstrated that the old principles were unnatural and unreal, men began to act as if this were not so. Individuals began to gather under the old banners, and, what was worse, they were not motivated by any strict adherence to principle but 'as their prejudices ... their inclinations, or other motives ... directed them';[26] former tories were enrolled as whigs and vice versa.

The factions re-established old controversies; individuals, in opposition to each other but temporarily united in 1688, parted once again. 'Danger to the church, on one side, and danger to the state on the other, were apprehended from men who meant no harm to either; ... it is a certain truth, that the struggle was in the main for power, not principle.'[27] Here is the key to Bolingbroke's whole account of the rise of party. In his view one can at least assume that the old pre-revolutionary parties had some principles, that the great national party of the revolution even acted exclusively on principle; but the post-revolutionary parties were more concerned with power than with any principle at all. This last view is a severe indictment indeed, and it is the more revealing when it is remembered that it is in this particular epoch and arena that Bolingbroke himself operated.

His historical account of the rise and development of political parties, in the *Dissertation upon Parties*, concludes at this point, but a perusal of some of his other writings will carry the story a little further. The first great national crisis facing the country after the revolution was the whole question of the succession. As long as Anne's son, the Duke of Gloucester, survived, there was no problem; but upon his death a new solution had to be found, and this became a party issue. When the succession of the House of Hanover was proposed the tories were clearly not over-enthusiastic. The 'tories voted for it then; and the acts that were judged necessary to secure it, some of them at least, were proposed by them', but they only supported it because 'there was no other safe and practicable'.[28] This notable lack of enthusiasm Bolingbroke attributed to the power of the Jacobite faction. The whigs on the other hand were enthusiastic for the Hanoverian succession, though not for the right reasons. They certainly acted as a national party 'and adhered to this settlement of the crown with a distinguished zeal',[29] but unfortunately the national interest of protestantism and liberty, trumpeted by the whigs as their only interest, was in fact a secondary concern, 'and the cause of succession was supported more for the sake of party or faction, than for the sake of the nation, and with views that went more directly to the establishment of their own administration, than to a solid settlement of the present [Hanoverian] family'.[30]

As if men had not been foolish enough over this issue, they showed still less wisdom as time progressed. The war with France provoked yet further the spirit of factionalism, though at first 'the disposition of the nation was absolutely turned to a war with France, on the death of king James the Second, by the acknowledgment Louis the Fourteenth made of his son as king of England'.[31] The spirit of national accord on this was soon dissipated by faction and discord, so that patriotism and war became the doubtful privilege of the whigs alone. In adopting a belligerent foreign policy, the whigs acted 'without a just and sober regard, such as one contemplates in their true light and sees them in their true magnitude, to the general system of power in Europe; and, in short, with a principal regard merely to particular interests at home and abroad. I say at home and abroad: because it is not less true, that they have sacrificed the wealth of their country to the forming and maintaining, beyond all pretences of necessity, alliances abroad.'[32] In the whig party itself men of various connections and groups may have coalesced in order to weave together the strands of faction and dissent. But in the country as a whole there was no national party at all; the body politic had, as it were, developed a perpetual squint. 'The two parties were in truth become factions in the strict sense of the word.'[33]

Party violence continued, extending in all directions, and reached its climax in the whig prosecution of Sacheverell, the tory cleric. This was followed by a change of ministry. But the tories assumed power in 1710 'in the same dispositions as all parties have done; that the principal spring of our actions was to have the government of the State in our hands; that our principal views were the conservation of this power, great employments to ourselves, and great opportunities of rewarding those who had helped to raise us, and of hurting those who stood in opposition to us'.[34]

Power politics clearly dominated the scene, and principles were as puppets on strings. But what, we may ask, were the tory principles or precepts at this time? The whole trend of government from 1688 to 1710 had been bad, in Bolingbroke's opinion, for it had loosened 'the bond of our constitution in church and state'.[35] In this situation it was assumed that the true men of merit—the landed interest—supported the tories, while the whigs were merely the remnants of the old exclusionists supported by dissenters and the moneyed classes. The tories proposed to maintain their power by supporting the royal influence especially through the church, by filling all civil service posts with loyal men, and by appealing to the innate conservatism of society as a whole.

Unfortunately for them, their leaders—and in particular Oxford—could not compose an enduring ministry on such vague generalities, and their leadership increasingly spent its energy on clinging to office rather than on devising a system of principles. The tory party *qua* party in fact did not exist as a body but as a collection of factions held together only by the external pressure of that other faction, the whigs. Amid the shifting sands of contemporary politics, 'The peace [of Utrecht] had been judged with reason to be the only solid foundation whereupon we could erect a tory system'.[36] But even this did not gain the solid support of the party. The Whimsicals, as Bolingbroke christened the Hanoverian tories, were not even willing to support their party. The succession question arose anew, and both parties exploited it for the purposes of retaining or acquiring power. Both of them 'pretended equally to have the national interest at heart, yet the national interest was so plainly on one side of the question, and the other side was so plainly partial, at the expense of this interest'.[37] The whigs gave it out that the Hanoverians were committed to their cause, while the Jacobites asserted that the protestant succession meant that only whigs would have power and all honest men would be dispossessed.

Such was the state of the parties when Anne died. With the accession of George I the whigs assumed office; 'the whole fury of party'[38] was let loose and they proceeded to 'proscribe in effect every man in the country who did not bear the name of whig'. The tories, devoid of inward convictions, 'began soon to act like men delivered over to their passions, and unguided by any other principle'.[39] Under these pressures the fabric of the party crumbled, and its members dispersed, some to become Jacobites, some Whimsicals, and some crypto-whigs. Of those who remained, the 'tories who had been true to one another to the last were an handful, and no great vigour could be expected from them'.[40] The party was leaderless; Oxford was impeached and imprisoned; Bolingbroke was a proscribed traitor and an exile.

In the *Dissertation upon Parties* Bolingbroke examines parties in the decade after 1715 to see their state in his own time. He establishes to his own satisfaction that the whole party system has now completely decayed, and all that remains is a set of factions which bear no resemblance to the older parties before 1688 or even before 1715.

> One possible division, then, is that of men angry with the government, and yet resolved to maintain the constitution. . . . A second possible division is that of men averse to the government, because they are so to the constitution, . . . or averse to the constitution, because they are so to the government, that they might change the constitution. The other would sacrifice the constitution, that they might subvert the government. A third division . . . is that of men attached to the government; or to speak more properly still, to the power, profit, or protection they acquire by the favour of these persons, but enemies to the constitution.[41]

The first division of men hostile to the government but not to the constitution is singularly harmless to society because these men are willing to act within the law, to gain a following and then to put their policies in action. Such men can scarcely be called factional, though they may be disruptive in so far as they refuse to support the current national party. The second group are the extremists who will not work the constitution as it stands. Such in Bolingbroke's day are the Jacobites, and their influence, save on rare occasions, may be reckoned as slight indeed. The third group are the creators and supporters of political parties who seek to destroy the constitution which curbs their political self-indulgence. They are in particular the men who support such figures as Walpole: men who would undermine liberty simply because they have affection only for themselves and act only in their interest.

The methods by means of which such a party flourishes, as described by Bolingbroke, are most ingenious (and not dissimilar to the stratagems which would apply in our own time). First, they seek to recruit a large military establishment, ostensibly for defence, but in

reality to overawe the public and prevent any open criticism of their
activity. This is the classic means of establishing a tyranny, *à la*
Peisistratus. Secondly, they conjure up enemies abroad for the purpose
of obtaining 'new powers, or for straining old ones';[42] and would
frighten the public into supporting their nefarious activities.

The fount of their power is heightened and ultimately guaranteed
by the corruption of the legislature. 'By the corruption of parliament,
and the absolute influence of a king, or his minister, on the two houses,
we return into that state, to deliver or secure us from which parliaments
were instituted, and are really governed by the arbitrary will of one
man. Our whole constitution is at once dissolved.'[43] Once parliament
(like the radio station in modern revolutions) is secured, all other things
are felt to be unimportant. Parliament is the outward garb that makes
tyranny presentable. 'No tyranny can be more severe than that which
is exercised by a concert with a parliament.'[44] Parliaments need not be
abolished if the executive can control them, because the outward forms
may continue quite happily while tyranny ensconces itself. The tyrant
who controls parliament need not be one 'in the gross, when he can be
so in detail; nor in name when he can be so in effect'.[45] Control of
parliament is ensured by corruption, which 'serves to oil the wheels of
government and to render the administration more smooth and easy'.[46]
Corruption is the means by which the third division or faction maintains itself and destroys the national party.

The policies adopted by this faction will include the promotion of
a civil list of great size to release the executive from dependence on
parliament. At the same time it will bring about an increase of expenditure and with it heavier taxation. This policy will help to destroy the
country's predisposition to frugality, which will be another step in the
total corruption of the state. It will 'impoverish the people . . . render
them submissive . . . beggar them out of their sturdiness'.[47] The yeo-
man will become a serf but the executive will be more free; the
bureaucracy will be greater and speculation will destroy national
confidence. In other words, Bolingbroke is propounding the thesis that
the party has become a great factional machine, devoted and dedicated
to its own self-preservation and the destruction of all else.

The only hope is to destroy such a leviathan of a faction. What is
to be done? Bolingbroke offers the following suggestions.

> They who affect to head an opposition, or to make any con-
> siderable figure in it, must be equal, at least, to those whom they

oppose; I do not say, in parts only, but in application and industry, and the fruits of both, information and knowledge, and a certain preparedness for all events that may arise. Every administration is a system of conduct: opposition, therefore, should be a system of conduct likewise: an opposite, but not a dependent system. . . . they who engage in opposition, are under as great obligations to prepare themselves to control, as they who serve the crown are under to prepare themselves to carry on, the administration: and that a party, formed for this purpose . . . do not act like wise men, unless they act systematically, and unless they contrast, on every occasion, that scheme of policy which the public interest requires to be followed, with that which is suited to no interest but the private interest of the prince or his ministers. . . . I presume there is no need of labouring to prove, that a party who opposed, systematically, a wise to a silly, an honest to an iniquitous, scheme of government, would acquire greater reputation and strength, and arrive more surely at their end, than a party who opposed, occasionally as it were, without any common system, without any general concert, with little uniformity, little preservation, little perseverance, and as little knowledge or political capacity.[48]

Yet opposition alone cannot destroy those factions which Bolingbroke abominates, because opposition as such is a technique rather than a constructive power.

It therefore behoves the 'friends of liberty to lay aside the groundless distinctions, which are employed to amuse and betray them; let them continue to coalite; let them hold fast their integrity, and support with spirit and perseverance the cause of their country, and they will confirm the good, reclaim the bad, vanquish the incorrigible, and . . . triumph, even over corruption'.[49] This will see the creation or restoration of the national party which will usher in the new age.

Bolingbroke simply accepts 'that division has caused all the mischief we lament, that union can alone retrieve it, and that . . . such a union can never be expected till . . . faction be banished from the administration'.[50] The country party must reappear for it is the only true party of the past, the present, or the future. It is the only party which represents completely all segments of society, and it alone is the party whose history will be worth recording, all others are factions and are best forgotten.

On 'The Patriot King'

All the world knows that I never did begin a war with the two Houses of Parliament. . . . I never did intend to encroach upon their privileges. . . . You will never do right until you give God his due, the King his due . . . and the people their due. . . . For the people I desire their liberty and freedom as much as anybody whatever. . . . But I must tell you that their liberty and freedom consist in having of government: those laws by which their life and their goods may be most their own. It is not having a share in government, that is nothing pertaining to them. A subject and a sovereign are clean different things.

CHARLES II

JUST as it has been traditional to regard Machiavelli's writings as the works of the devil, so Bolingbroke's *Idea of a Patriot King* has been considered the *summum malum* of George III's false political precepts. That king is considered to have been nourished exclusively upon this and other works of Bolingbroke, and to have learned his lessons so well that he attempted a restoration of monarchical power and influence, with a concomitant diminution of parliamentary authority, in accordance with the teaching of this tory philosopher.* In fact this was not the case; it is very doubtful if George III had ever read Bolingbroke's works,† although some members

---

* This view of the influence of Bolingbroke on George III probably originated with Horace Walpole. It was taken up by whiggishly inclined historians to become one of the clichés of English history.

† J. Steven Watson dismisses this old idea in his *The Reign of George III* (Oxford, 1960), p. 6. Most modern historians would agree that the king did not need

of his royal entourage may have done so and then insinuated Bolingbroke's ideas into the royal mind. Nevertheless, the myth remains that George III was a bad king because he subverted the virtuous parliament, and that he was instructed in this by Bolingbroke. Consequently Bolingbroke is to be regarded, in the words of the authors of *1066 And All That*, as 'a bad thing'.

As a result of the popular myth, the *Idea of a Patriot King* has retained this dubious reputation. It is referred to for the most part in disparaging terms, chiefly by those who have given it no more than a cursory reading. The intentions of the author are entirely obscured, and it is used as part of the evidence for the failure of the 'Constitutional Experiment'. It should, however, be considered differently. It was the most obviously utopian work that Bolingbroke was ever to write. At its best it can stand worthily with the many writings from Plato to the present day on the hoped-for utopia; for the rest, it is a polemical broadside in the campaign against Walpole. Thus it has on two counts a proper place in political literature, and should not be assigned the alien rôle of Hanoverian scapegoat.

This work of Bolingbroke is not original, nor is it something special in the whole line of writings of his time. It is obviously patterned on Machiavelli's *The Prince*, while it contains ideas gleaned from the writings of such diverse figures as Plato and Davenant. It is a whig, not a tory, document. It also repeats much that Bolingbroke says elsewhere. On the other hand, it is a more precise and definitive statement of his ideal government than any he had previously formulated.

The work was dedicated to Frederick, Prince of Wales, the eldest son of George II. This prince, like his father before him, had quarrelled with his father and had become the leader of the malcontents who harassed the leaders of the government. Prince Frederick's was a most unattractive character. His former tutor described him thus: 'He has the most vicious nature and the most false heart that ever man had, nor are his vices the vices of a gentleman, but the mean tricks of a knavish footman.' Prince Frederick was more memorable dead than alive.[1]

> Here lies Fred
> Who was alive and is dead:

---

to read Bolingbroke, for 'Young George aimed at no more power than his grandfather.... He meant ... to show the world that the reign of virtue had begun'—and that was all.

Had it been his father,
I had much rather;
Had it been his brother,
Still better than another;
Had it been his sister
No one would have missed her;
Had it been the whole generation,
Still better for the nation:
Who was alive and is dead,—
There's no more to be said.*

Although this prince was weak, and Bolingbroke could scarcely have been sincere in his admiration of him, he was nevertheless the centre of the opposition and therefore an important factor in the calculations and ambitions of opposition leaders. That Bolingbroke saw in him the potential Patriot King is inconceivable. What attracted Bolingbroke was the practical usefulness of the prince's position, not his potentialities as a ruler.

It is to be doubted whether Bolingbroke's motivations ever arose above those of sheer expediency. In this essay he claims, in a high-flown exordium, that he intends 'to reinfuse the spirit of liberty, to reform the morals, and to raise the sentiments of the people'.[2] But these gushings from his pen do not really become him at all. This planned restoration of the golden age can only occur with 'the concurrence and influence of a patriot king'[3] assisted by men of virtue—and 'men of virtue' writ large spells out the name of Henry St John, Viscount Bolingbroke. Even so, like many political tracts (Machiavelli's *Prince*, for example) written to promote a particularist interest, the *Patriot King* has more than an ephemeral significance. With an author of so varied and rich a mind as Bolingbroke, the argument is capable of rising from the specific to the general, and of giving the essay a justifiable place in the literature of political theory.

To delineate the rôle of the Patriot King is no simple task. Even to disinter from history the origins of ordinary kingship is difficult, let alone those of Patriot Kingship. Some idea of the origin and nature of ordinary kingship as seen by Bolingbroke is essential in order that the rôle of the Patriot King should be properly understood. In the first

* This epitaph was composed by the Jacobites and it is a variant on one composed for Lord Clarendon; *cf.* Averyl Edwards. *Frederick Louis, Prince of Wales* (London, 1947), pp. 188-9.

place, it has to be realised that, for Bolingbroke, kings do not have divine rights in their creation, in their powers or in themselves. This rejection of divine right is an essential part of Bolingbroke's whole approach and is a necessary foundation for his conceptual framework. The perversion of the concept of kingship stems, he considers, from the ancient priestly function of the ruler. When the priesthood discovered the surest way to maintain their powers was to be associated with the priest-king, they then postulated the divine right of the king who happened coincidentally to be their presiding officer. In other words, by the creation of a divinely authorised ruler, the priestly class, particularly in the post-Hellenistic era, ensured their authority. Such an over-simplification of the despised divine-right principle, confounding its origins with the subsequent misuse of it, is, of course, a further expression of Bolingbroke's rationalistic sentiments. He preferred a more empirical basis for the origin of his executive, playing the rôle, not of the idealist philosopher acting as the law-giver, but rather of the law-giver making recourse to a pragmatic philosophy.

Despite all that Bolingbroke had done in his active political life, and all the diverse platforms upon which he had constructed his career, it is quite certain that he never seriously supported the high-flying pretensions of the Caroline monarchy. If he had wanted to restore the legitimate monarchy, it was with the intention of basing it within the accepted constitutional framework, not upon the oracular claims of a *vox et praeterea nihil*. Not for him were the absolutisms of Europe, if only because an exalted monarchy would inevitably involve a diminution of that ministerial power and prestige which, at the end of Anne's reign, he enjoyed and which ever after he yearned to regain. Hence, even in his utopia, he was careful to base his concept of kingship firmly in this world and not in the hereafter.

In ancient times, he observes, the established kings had been reverenced both alive and dead. 'Majesty was the first, and divinity the second reward.'[4] But what was the source of 'Majesty'? It came to a particular individual because he had been chosen by the community to lead and to guide. If he had been good he was enshrined to ensure his continual beneficence when dead. Further, as the king personified the state, the state religion was certain to centre round the king, and it was then hard to distinguish between 'Roma et Augustus'. Once a royal dynasty had been established it continued to reap the reward granted to its founder, and to acquire accordingly a prescriptive merit. Each successive king was in a sense a reincarnation of the founder and acquired the charismatic qualities associated with the original ruler. Hence in the middle ages English kings were not slow to exploit their relationship with one of the national saints, Edward the Confessor, claiming as an outward sign of this their ability to touch for the King's Evil. This manifestation of sanctity reappeared in all the English monarchs until the death of Queen Anne. It was perfectly obvious that her successors, although connected to the legitimate line, were sovereigns by consent of the legislature and so perhaps lacked the special sanctions which would have been theirs had they been of the direct line.

As a result, therefore, of the authority and aura of antiquity which mantled the royal family, bad sovereigns were endured, although reason might well have dictated their overthrow. Even when revolutions took place and monarchs were deposed, the idea of monarchy continued. Bolingbroke recognises that the basis for monarchy was not entirely in accord with reason; but to suggest an alternative to monarchy was to risk the outright rejection of his projects. The memory of the republican experiment in the 1650s was still painfully fresh, and republicanism was held in opprobrium. Any non-monarchical state, however rational, must be a form of republicanism, and republicanism was too radical a system to be acceptable to the majority of Englishmen.

Lest there be any doubts as to where he stood on this question, Bolingbroke states that he esteems 'monarchy above any form of government, and hereditary monarchy above elective'.[5] He seeks thereby to avoid rousing the fears of the particular class and segment of society to whom he directs his writings. His support of the hereditary principle should not, of course, obscure his belief that all monarchies depend to some extent upon election. If a monarch is to succeed he must have the support of a sizeable proportion of the population, though in default of active support he may survive, given a failure to oppose on the part of the people. Despite the fact that no formal election actually occurs, the national act of submission and homage can be regarded as a ratification of the election or selection of the monarch. If one goes further and consents to any alteration in the succession, such as preferring the male to the female, then one is in a sense choosing or electing.

While God has not ordained any particular form of government—having instituted 'neither monarchy, nor aristocracy',[6] nor mixed government—man is subject to human law which has the sanction of divine law. Once a community is established and its form of government fixed, the very act of establishment implies divine approval, for would God allow anything to be created if He did not approve of it? Therefore, as the institution of government and law is the concern of God, man is morally bound to follow the human law which is the outward manifestation of divine law. Obviously, if a king succeeds to the throne, then his subjects must obey him. But arguing thus is not an endorsement of Caroline divine right; rather it implies a 'divine right to govern well, and conformably to the constitution'.[7] Bolingbroke strongly maintains that monarchs do not have powers by their mere existence as rulers, but only in accordance with some set of accepted laws. Bad kings there may be, and in fact they are probably inevitable, but their badness cannot be condoned by pretensions to divine authority.

The only kings with such authority and protection are those who govern by reason and justice which are projections of a divine order and will. Their fulfilment or otherwise of divine precepts may be measured by the happiness engendered by their reigns. 'God has made us to desire happiness; He has made our happiness dependent on society; and the happiness of society dependent on good or bad government.'[8] In the *Republic* Plato gives as his final definition of the ruler who must be obeyed, one who cares for the happiness of the whole society, and he supports this thesis in the *Politicus* and *Crito*. Thus, the only good kings are those who can be known to have brought happiness to their subjects. Of course, the whole concept rests on the definition of happiness itself, and to conceive happiness as something externally conditioned is impossible. The ideal king might therefore be redefined as one who does not make his people unhappy. Moreover, hell is easier for the human mind to conceive than heaven, and so absolute misery is easier to define than absolute bliss.

Bolingbroke's invoking the 'right of happiness' has interesting implications. Pursuing his argument, one can contend, for example, that George III, in making his American subjects unhappy, as it seemed to them, was not subscribing to the main precept for which government was established, namely happiness. It would therefore follow that some new government could legitimately be established which would produce the requisite degree of happiness. Jefferson and his associates exploited this argument to justify their rebellion. This 'right of happiness' is a very important concept in political theory. It is measurable, however, only in the long unfolding of history, and an immediate unhappiness may be a necessary phase in the ultimate process of gaining the *summum bonum*. Consequently it is not obvious that the aim of immediate happiness is sufficient justification for revolution, and, unfortunately the problem has been obscured by the failure to ascertain the true relationship between happiness and duty, or between what is pleasurable and what is right.

Kings, Bolingbroke considers, have divine rights solely as the agents of God; reverence for kings as though they were immortal 'is preposterous and repugnant to common sense'.[9] Proper respect, however, for those in authority is mandatory, for the man in office represents a corporate personality greater than the mere sum of the component parts of society. But the excessive adulation of the man in office *qua* man leads only to the extravagances of tyranny. It is absurd to assume, as was the case, for example, in the orientalised Roman imperial state, that as the gods are infallible, even so the sovereign as *Divus Caesar* is infallible. The office may be divinely appointed, but this does not confer divinity upon the holder of the office. Such extravagances are extreme, according to Bolingbroke. A kingdom does not exist for the king, but on the contrary, an earthly kingdom exists in the light of the heavenly kingdom; 'majesty is not an inherent, but a reflected light'.[10] A king may embody the state, but the state itself must be distinguished from the king and from the agencies of its own authority. Men are mortal; gods are divine; the charisma of the gods is not the hereditary mantle of human rulers seeking apotheosis.

Hereditary monarchies, indeed, are no more sacred than elective ones, and on purely rational grounds the elective monarchy might seem to have more elements of the sacred than the hereditary. Each election, Bolingbroke, thinks would in a sense seek out by purely rational means that single individual in the state who possessed most of the divine qualities of the first king. Selection merely through the circumstance of birth alone gives a wide margin for error. Unfortunately, he observes, the appointed time for royal elections is not a set time designated by a written constitution but an hour fixed by the inscrutable will of providence; and by an unhappy coincidence the royal elections seem always to occur at a time of national distress or calamity. Instead of calm reason presiding over the choice, the elections are often dominated by the furies, avenging the sins of the previous reign. The worst of men rather than the best seem to prevail in the contest. Even with the election of the best possible candidate, the events surrounding his election may have been so complicated, and so discouraging, that with the best will in the world his efforts for future success will be hampered and frustrated.[11]

In hereditary monarchies, Bolingbroke notes, the king's demise cannot be predicted with any greater degree of certainty than in an elected one, but his death is of less consequence. Each king is one of an unbroken line; 'the king is dead, long live the king'; there is no interregnum. The individual dies but the national personality which he represents continues. The authority of history, the lustre of antiquity, and the magnetism of charismatic power are all attributed to the new sovereign; people and king are clathrated in a common tradition. The hereditary monarchy is an immortal monarchy, and since it participates in the immortal it reflects a fundamental aspiration of man. Hereditary kings may be assassinated, they may die in battle, and the state may lapse into chaos, but there is always one to follow, and this leads to a highly desirable element of stability. Internal chaos is often the result of insecure succession. If one must have a monarchy—and Bolingbroke assumes that this is the best form of government—then the chances and changes of human life would certainly suggest that an hereditary monarchy is preferable and less liable to cause the disorder and acute unhappiness of a disputed succession.

The monarchy itself may be immortal, but the definition of kingship is not immutable, and may be altered according to the needs of the age. History demonstrates that kings may hold total sway over their subjects, or be totally subject to their people's will. It is believed, however, that monarchy, when truly defined, will always promote the liberty of the people. It should be observed that, on this basis, what is conceived of as the liberty of the people may change but it does not mean the end of monarchy. The modern constitutional monarchy, shorn of all autocratic powers, stripped 'naked, as it were and left with a few tattered rags to clothe its majesty',[12] still has a useful function to perform in the government and still to some degree provides the balance in society. The constitutional king can by his mere existence go far to protect the people from the potential machinations of evil men, simply because the sovereign prevents these malefactors from assuming that final 'absolute, unlimited, and uncontrollable power'[13] which is the essential core of tyranny.

Bolingbroke insists that all kings should rule by law and be subject to law. To him a balanced government is the best government, and monarchy tends to maintain and establish the necessary balance between democracy and aristocracy. The government containing all of these elements will fulfil the basic requirements for good government. A balanced government precludes absolutism. Monarchy is not, he says, synonymous with absolutism since 'to constitute monarchy, or the government of a single person, it is not necessary that this power'— namely the absolute, unlimited and uncontrolled power that exists potentially in every state—'should be lodged in the monarch alone'.[14] Power is to be shared by the monarch with the elements which establish the good government.

The advocates in the seventeenth century of 'mixed monarchy' would have found this quite acceptable. In addition to this, Bolingbroke, with perhaps a subconscious debt to the deists, does not hesitate to apply his doctrine of limitation even to God, Who, he noted, is 'limited by the rule which infinite wisdom prescribes to infinite power'.[15] In Bolingbroke's eyes, the impatient Jehovah of the Old Testament was not always in harmony with the best balanced world; but the God of the New Testament, generally speaking, was a God whose power was blended by reason into a harmonious balance. Assuming that God is thus limited—and He certainly was to the deist theologians whose doctrines Bolingbroke shared—then *a fortiori* there were limits ascribed to the power of human sovereigns who were but creatures of God. 'Majesty is not an inherent but a reflected light.'[16]

Can limitations on sovereignty be so devised that liberty will be preserved and yet allow the Crown the necessary authority to govern efficiently? The contemporary theorist would reply in the affirmative, and so would Bolingbroke. Rules may be so established that the bad prince will be limited in his authority, which will enable the people to remain free, but these rules need not be so restricting that a good prince is unable to act effectively. In fact Bolingbroke could point to a society and a state that had done this; he considered that the British constitution of his own day had reached a level of perfection that could hardly be improved. The evil monarch was shackled, the good one was unchained. No king

> who is not, in the true meaning of the word, a patriot, can govern Britain with ease, security, honour, dignity, or indeed with sufficient strength. But yet a king, who is a patriot, may govern with all the former; and besides them, with power as extended as the most absolute monarch can boast, and a power,

too, far more agreeable in the enjoyment, as well as more effectual in the operation.[17]

What applied in Britain could apply elsewhere; the model existed and copies could be made at will. Bolingbroke was not unlike Bentham in his ingenuousness concerning human nature and its forms of government, but to confirm the general feasibility of his views regarding a 'patriot's' powers one might cite the age of Victoria. Queen Victoria was in many ways a 'patriot' monarch, and although her apparent powers were far more limited than those of many other contemporary sovereigns, she had vast influence and prestige. Other rulers apparently so *vollmächtig* made much less of an impression upon their era than she did. Of course, critics will reply that Victoria herself had little or nothing to do with it since economic forces, imperialism and so forth were the real sources of the importance of her reign. Yet to the popular mind these intangibles were represented by a person, and the queen was credited with the successes of her country. And to some degree the popular mind was right, for she set a pattern, a pattern of stability and an image of authority which sanctioned the power of the people of whom she was the symbol.

The key word is 'patriot'. After the vociferous clamourings of nationalism, the domestic violence and the slaughter of mankind which has taken place under the mantle of patriotism, our use of the word has a kind of jaded quality. But in the better sense of the word, the patriot is one whose life is directed by 'great principles and supported by great virtues';[18] the true patriot is also the truly good man. Without patriotism in this latter sense no man, be he sovereign or subject, can be properly esteemed great; in fact, without this guiding philosophy he cannot even attempt greatness. Unless an incurable cynic, or an ardent supporter of the hobbesian natural man, one will concede that most sovereigns have within themselves a potential greatness, though this is a frail plant and must be tended with great care.

To Bolingbroke the agent in the destruction of the true spirit of patriotism is the insidious nature of flattery. Flattery he knows surrounds all men and particularly those placed in high office. Princes, he affirms, are the most vulnerable since from birth they hold a place of honour and esteem, so that a constant guard must be kept lest through flattery they are inculcated with a belief that they are not as other men. Once they assume this to be the case, they have lost the real character of patriots. The wise prince, according to Bolingbroke, must constantly be inspired with a real awareness and perception of what is genuine and what is false, and he should recognise that each flattering remark is an attempt to wean him from his principles. He conceives that the real destroyers of Louis XIV as an individual and as a statesman were not foreign wars, licentious living and failures of domestic policy, as a good many historians would have us believe, but rather his own entourage at court. These persons induced him to believe that he was always right, or rather that he was never wrong. Bolingbroke says that such gross flattery ruined the character of one who might otherwise have been a great patriot. Applause should be given for worthy acts, but it should not be showered indiscriminately as by the sycophant.

If a sovereign exists, he does not exist by himself. 'The prince and the people take, in effect, a sort of engagement with one another; the prince to govern well, the people to honour and obey him.'[19] Despite any contrary theory that Bolingbroke may have expressed elsewhere—and in his *Fragments* he certainly goes far to repudiate the implications of this idea—he does assert in *The Patriot King* that there is some sort of contract between sovereign and subject. If a contract exists, then clearly there are obligations on both sides, and the idea of contract, however vaguely presented, is yet a further refutation of the idea of divine right. It is true that, assuming an hereditary monarchy, the engagement between prince and people may only be *pro forma*; but an alert people, confident and secure in their liberty, will take every precaution to prevent the usurpation of their sovereignty and any basic alteration of the contract. No people should be so foolish as to alter the engagement themselves by extending the powers of a prince in the pious hope that the prince will somehow be filled with gratitude and not try to overthrow the contract completely. He will inevitably recognise the weakness of his subjects and, unless he be very much the patriot, exploit that weakness by becoming a tyrant. If tyranny ensues, then all possible means may be used by the people to obstruct the tyranny and to restore the contract. Bolingbroke implies that constitutional means should be used for obstructing the tyranny, but in his *Dissertation upon Parties* he follows Locke in allowing the right of revolution, and there is no indication that here in the *Patriot King* he has contrary opinions.

However, it is not right, he believes, to embark upon such a fateful course except in the most disastrous of situations. In ordinary circumstances the people would have asserted their rights long before a real tyranny had developed and the prince would respect their views. Princes like other men soon see where their true interests lie, and if they can see clearly that it is in their interest to play the patriot then they will do so. Of course, not all princes can achieve true patriotism, because of their youth, their inexperience or their general incompetence; but their attempts to be patriots should receive both the assistance and the applause of their subjects. The patriot prince and the free subject will be united. This good union 'will blast many a wicked project, keep virtue in countenance, and vice to some degree at least in awe'.[20] Even though circumstances might arise when both king and people are victimised, this affliction might well be the necessary chastisement for indifference and, once overcome, might unite the state the more firmly. Great sorrow often unites mankind more easily than great joy.

But the search for or the creation of the Patriot King may be as chimerical as Diogenes' search for the honest man. Humanity being what it is—overcome with inertia and congenitally reluctant to change —it is quite possible that no search will be made at all. But if there be a sign that such a search is for the benefit of society, men will hasten to alter their course and act. The true prince will arise. He will, Boling-broke believes, adopt virtue by self-interest (though it is to be doubted whether the principle of self-interest is compatible with the emergence of a 'sign' of selfless patriotism benefiting society and not the self). If, however, a sign is given, the wise prince whose state has been corrupted will now see that further corruption is against his interest. He will begin to realise the benefits that accrue from patriotism for himself and for his people, and will not revert to tyranny. Enlightened self-interest will become the enlightened selfless interest of the true patriot. Narrow interest will give way to the *summum bonum*. What is more, expediency will be replaced by a duty to the whole of society, and the patriot will follow his course of action because 'it is his duty to do so; a duty that he owes to God by one law, and to his people by another'.[21]

Government is to be established on a principle of mutual obligation. Men, it appears, cannot live apart from one another, because the communal instinct is a part of their very being. Anarchy is unsatisfactory, for it represents disorder, and order is the proper end of nature. With the creation of government—so ran the notion current in the eighteenth century—some individual liberty had to be surrendered, but this indicated a loss of independence rather than a loss of freedom. It implied the disappearance of licence and the prevention of tyranny: the belief, in fact, that good government aids liberty under the law— the best liberty—and that legal liberty promotes good government.

The government acts in accordance with the rights of sovereign and people, all apportioned in harmony. The Patriot King will act virtuously as the leader of the government because he is bound to do so by God's law and by the concept of the 'engagement'. He 'will make one, and but one, distinction between his rights and those of his people; he will look upon his to be a trust, and theirs a property'.[22] A trust is not owned but enjoyed, not to be wrongly augmented or dissipated; and property is perpetual, to be kept intact for posterity. The trust and the property are one and can never be divided. The Patriot King will 'discern, that he can have no more than is trusted to him by the constitution; and that his people, who had an original right to the whole by the law of nature, can have the sole indefeasible right to any part; really have such a right to that part which they have reserved to themselves'.[23] Thus Bolingbroke takes a firm stand against any doctrine which maintains that the people have no rights but only privileges.

The alteration of the succession and the choice of a new dynasty do not change the relationship of king and people. The king is the king with his rights defined by the law of nature and of reason; the idea of 'king' is constant, but the man as king is not. It is he who is changed, not the office. In the choice of the prince the people have a part to play, and though he may succeed by hereditary succession, his accession requires popular approval. Each king is re-enacting in his enthronement the initial selection of the founder of the dynasty. 'Royal blood can give no right, nor length of succession any prescription, against the constitution.'[24] This affirms the rights of the people acting within the original constitution, and acknowledges that the induction of a truly Patriot King, which, properly expresses the views of the people, is valid. The Patriot King

> must be a patriot from the first. He must be such in resolution before he grows such in practice. He must fix at once the general principles and ends of all his actions, and determine that his whole conduct shall be regulated by them, and directed to them. When he has done this, he will have turned, by one great effort, the best of his mind so strongly towards the perfection of a kindly character, that he will exercise with ease, as it were by a natural determination, all the virtues of it; which will be suggested to him on every occasion by the principles wherewith his mind is involved, and by those ends that are constant objects of his attention.[25]

What specifically are the virtues that Bolingbroke's Patriot King must exercise to maintain liberty, and to create or re-establish the freedom of the constitution? What does he mean by these terms? Liberty is the possession by the people of their 'property' and the king his 'trust'. The freedom of the constitution, much as Machiavelli saw it, might be said to depend upon 'not only the forms and customs, but the different classes and powers and privileges attributed to them, which are established in the state'.[26] And to these must be added something not tangible, namely a particular character and spirit of the people. A harmonious blending between this national spirit and the possession of 'property' and 'trust'—the powers of the different classes—is essential for the well-being of the state. Perfection is attained when all are in harmonious balance. True liberty cannot be lost if the national spirit retains its purity; even if force be used the character and spirit will not be permanently changed and the concept of freedom will not be obliterated. However, if some method can be devised to change the spirit and character of the people, then the freedom of the constitution can be subverted, its essential balance can be lost and liberty can disappear.

The chief method of subversion, Bolingbroke suggests, is the advance of material prosperity. He grants that it is well for a society to develop and improve itself to a high degree of material well-being, but he insists on the necessity of constant vigilance on behalf of freedom. Once a society attains security, becomes lavish and opulent, and loses its spiritual values, its liberties can be whittled away. The potential tyrant needs only to give his people riches and security, and then they are his for ever. Athenian virtue was surrendered to the temptations of wealth and power; the citizenry lost sight of what had made them an example to all men, and in grasping at the mirage of material and military superiority they lost their greatest possession: freedom and power over themselves. Similarly the virtuous Roman republic was corrupted into the most vicious of tyrannies. Bolingbroke's view is well expressed in Goldsmith's *Deserted Village*: 'Ill fares the land, to hast'ning ills a prey, where wealth accumulates, and men decay.' Once the rot enters into the structure of society the most ruthless of measures are needed to halt it. If vice becomes virtue, lies truth, if once a people slides into a whirlpool of moral and physical destruction, such as Thucydides describes, then the national character, mind or spirit has been well-nigh lost. Unless drastic action be taken there will soon be no freedom, and, what is worse, the people will not care.

Dissimulation is the means by which the sovereign becomes a

tyrant, concealing his own beliefs because otherwise the people would take notice and his projects would be defeated. He acts, therefore, with such apparent mildness that his subjects do not see the direction he is taking. Bolingbroke is quite aware that corruption is more difficult in a society where the sovereign is highly esteemed, because this very esteem convinces the wise men that he could influence them unduly, and this puts them on their guard. The geese sleep when they have nothing to fear, and they fear nothing when the prince is apparently without influence, or even despised a little, so that he seems incapable of playing the tyrant. Yet it is the man assumed incompetent who, by craftily exploiting this situation, can gain great power. Most men cannot bring themselves to realise that by acting viciously or supporting venality under such a man they are in fact adding to his power. But each step which clouds the purity of the national spirit hastens the total collapse of the constitution, and finally when all have taken these steps, the whole society is corrupted; the spirit of the people is altered, and the tyrant can come into his own.

Should a state be in such a parlous condition its only hope is that a Patriot King will come to its rescue, though his arrival cannot be guaranteed to take place at the precise moment when he is needed. Some considerable period of tyranny may have to be borne and the 'utmost that private men can do, who remain untainted by the general contagion, is to keep the spirit of liberty alive in a few breasts; to protest against what they cannot hinder, and to claim on every occasion what they cannot by their own strength recover'.[27] Fortunately for mankind such men have always existed and even under persecution do not disappear. They and those whom they can influence await hungrily for the day of restoration. It is a day that often seems impossibly remote, but absolute tyranny does not persist for ever. A messiah will appear: that Patriot King who alone can command the respect and the authority necessary to bring the people back to liberty and to give them freedom, the freedom of the constitution.

One major element discerned by Bolingbroke in the corruption of the state is the dislocation of the orders within it. Once the balance between aristocracy and democracy, maintained by the king, has been upset, party and factions are encouraged to arise. The monarch is out of alignment with his people; it is his obligation to restore himself and them to harmony. Yet the task of repairing the state cannot be undertaken while corruption has any power, and a mere promulgation of new laws will not explicitly remedy the situation. Augustus' sumptuary legislation is a case in point. The Patriot King is aware of the danger of merely papering over the cracks, and knows that it is not just the form of the government that is in error but, more significantly, its spirit. Laws do not in themselves alter the spirit of a society, although they may be used to express and thus maintain that spirit. What the prince must do is to restore the spirit of liberty. If he be truly patriotic he should be able to do this so that the people may be brought back to their proper traditions. By design or by art he must root out corruption as a method of government, destroy its usefulness, and reinstate 'the orders and forms . . . to their primitive integrity, and become, what they were intended to be, real barriers against arbitrary power'.[28]

Bolingbroke is not just putting back the clock; rather he is saying that society, under good leadership, should recover and reassert the rights and privileges that it already has. There is in the whole of society, as a consequence of original sin, the tendency to evil, but this tendency need not dominate. If laxity has destroyed liberty, purity will recreate it. But laxity or vice is the easy way, while virtue is hard, so the Patriot King must exorcise the demon of self-indulgence and wield the sword of the redeeming spirit. Men inspired by this example will then discover that by doing good they will gain in power and authority, and by being good they will act anew in the proper spirit. 'A Patriot King is the most powerful of all reformers, for he is himself a sort of standing miracle, so rarely seen and so little understood, that the sure effects of his appearance will be admiration and love in every honest breast, confusion and terror to every guilty conscience, but submission and resignation in all. A new people will seem to arise with a new king.'[29]

Such a magical transformation will create the new race of heroes; a people changed out of all recognition when compared with their immediate predecessors. Having been tempted, having fallen and been redeemed, they will possess, like all those who have undergone conversion, a special character. Bolingbroke envisages a new Jerusalem and the return of the Davidic monarchy in the person of the Patriot King. But such a City of God is not found on earth, and regretfully he has to admit that the 'best instituted governments, like the best constituted animal bodies, carry in them the seeds of their own destruction; and though they grow and improve for a time, they will tend visibly to their dissolution'.[30] It is because society is healthy, because men prosper and all seems serene, that the watchfulness of the citizenry begins to falter. The society which has become affluent and secure is then once more liable to the evils which beset it before the advent of the Patriot King. 'Every hour they live is an hour less that they have to live.'[31] Society is seen by Bolingbroke as a living organism which is born, grows, and dies; nothing can be done permanently to halt its destruction. Suitable action, however, may postpone the hour of death, although an ultimate collapse cannot be prevented. Bolingbroke is certainly no optimist about mankind. Nevertheless he is sufficiently pragmatic to entertain hope for the present in the belief that the here and the now is of greater significance for the majority of men than some abstract future time. The efforts of the prince will be directed to repairing the damage caused by lesser men, and he will hope that by his actions the ship of state may be strong enough to weather the succeeding winds and waves.

No sovereign can cope with all eventualities, and his successors may not be true patriots. But at least he himself can be the patriot and serve as a model for future generations. It is assumed that the Patriot King would do everything in his power to ensure that his policies were followed by his immediate successor, but history teems with examples of the policy of one monarch being reversed by the king who succeeds him. The taking of all possible precautions against this would be no guarantee that this would not result. The Patriot King, however, must live his life doing his duty; and his people, when restored to liberty, will have the responsibility of preparing themselves for what is to come, good or ill. Having been revived by the leadership of their prince, the people should be able, for some time at least, to keep their freedoms intact. If they lose them again, it will be the result of their own folly.

Most of what has been said so far consists of generalisations, and Bolingbroke in his travels through the kingdom of philosophy has dallied in the province of Utopia. It is necessary to ask in what specific ways does the Patriot King resolve the dilemmas posed by the corrupted society? A dissertation upon sickness is interesting, and may be valuable in itself, but knowledge of a disease is not enough without some suggested methods of cure, or at least limitation.

Bolingbroke's first and most basic suggestion for the Patriot King is that he must in fact rule; he must rule personally and from the moment of his accession. There are to be no grand viziers, no shoguns in the realm; the king must be his own first minister. This is to prevent any individual or faction from gaining excessive power and dominating the state; the sovereign alone is to be the national leader. When a man is placed in authority, his worth—be he king or schoolmaster—is to no small measure determined by his first day, even his first hour, in power. He sets the tone for his administration, and this tone can have the greatest effect and consequences for the future. George III's mother seems to have been thinking on these lines when she gave him the advice: 'George be a king.' Public esteem is a powerful force, and if the sovereign enjoys it, his influence can be considerable. If his rôle is a positive one, commanding immediate respect from the people, then he may be able to exert great authority. Much of the character of the nineteenth century was derived from the rôle assumed by Queen Victoria and her court. Persons of known immoral character were banished, the proprieties were observed and the raffish, albeit amusing, world of the Regency disappeared to be replaced by the respectability of the Victorian era.

The decision to rule must be implemented with the help of wise advisers who support this premise. The sovereign will at once call to his side men of probity and wisdom whom he can trust to support his policies. If the previous sovereign has been weak, incompetent or tyrannical, the court will abound with vile men who have been the agents and creatures of corruption. These men will undoubtedly strive to retain their places and privileges, but if they see that the prince is firm in his resolution to begin anew, they will soon recognise that their time of power is at an end. They will, Bolingbroke says, be chased from the court as the money-changers were ejected by Christ from the temple. Bolingbroke, however, would not merely have these men dismissed: he would go further. He would hand them over to the courts for speedy trial and sentence; guilty as they so obviously are, their sentences will be richly deserved.

This hanging of fallen ministers because they were agents of the previous regime smacks of the purge, and suggests the principle of revenge and not of justice. There may, of course, be something in a little bloodletting: it may satisfy the populace, but it is likely to start a series of actions and set in train events which may make future policy difficult. The results of the cure may, in fact, be worse than the disease. The drawing up of proscription-lists of opponents is highly dangerous. Should it happen that by the turn of fortune's wheel those who are down and out get the upper hand, then the same fate would inevitably be meted out to their adversaries. Moreover, Bolingbroke almost falls into the error of executing for the sake of executing, or of acting, as

Voltaire so aptly put it upon the death of Admiral Byng, *pour encourager les autres*. He would even limit the royal clemency because clemency to be right must be used with rare discrimination. To cure the cancer in the state the surgery, he believes, must be complete, since any half-way measures may lead to the continuation of the disease. To restore the state corruption must be rooted out absolutely. The implication here is that to cure one must destroy; to begin anew one must pulverise the old; phoenix-like the good will rise from the ashes of the bad. Bolingbroke is drastic and draconian in his suggestions.

In addition to purging his council, the Patriot King will regulate the composition of his court. Many of those who hold ceremonial posts may have been the creatures of the previous regime and intimately associated with them in the public mind. The more notorious of them will be dismissed. Others who are relatively harmless can be persuaded to adhere to the new regime and thus be retained, especially if members of ancient families (Bolingbroke has a considerable antipathy to the *novus homo*). Tradition and traditional ceremonies are part of the magic of monarchy and are, Bolingbroke believes, the reflections of majesty, though not its reality. Those, therefore, who are content to be participants in the purely honorific aspects of kingship and are in most cases not sage enough to be considered as councillors should be retained. It is the wise prince who recognises this. Though persuaded that pageantry serves no utilitarian purpose, and is a 'despicable thing',[32] Bolingbroke is realistic enough to realise that the mystique of monarchy requires the maintenance of the purely ceremonial.

Once the knaves and fools have been ejected from office the prince will look for patriots to serve him. If possible he will call to his council men of known virtue and proven capacity. If, however, there has been a long period of decay, it will not be easy to discern such men. One possible group of advisers could be the opponents of the previous regime, but care will have to be taken that these men are not merely factious and have no deeper concerns than the pleasures of office. It is obvious that the new councillors should be men of wisdom and not merely cunning men. 'The cunning man knows how to pack the cards, the wise man how to play the game better; but it would be of no use to the first to pack the cards, if his knowledge stopped there, and he had no knowledge of the game; nor to the second to play the game better, if he did not know how to pack the cards, that he might unpack them by new shuffling. Inferior wisdom or cunning may get the better of folly; but superior wisdom will get the better of cunning.'[33]

The wise man may rightfully employ the arts of cunning and the wisdom of the serpent; he may use simulation or dissimulation in order to preserve the state and carry out his duties. Indeed, a little cunning is not dangerous, and is one of the tools of the wise man. But it should not become the only mode of acting, otherwise wisdom becomes tainted and the practitioner loses all the character of a statesman. The purely cunning man 'neither sees, nor is concerned to see, any further than his personal interests, and the support of his administration require'.[34] This is the minister who will ultimately defraud the people of their liberty, because his lowered standards will ensure that he can only act in this way and cannot be a true patriot.

Undoubtedly Bolingbroke, in attributing cunning to his opponents, thought of himself as the true patriot. 'The wise minister sees, and is concerned to see further . . . he sees the objects that are distant as well as those that are near . . . He thinks of fame as well as of applause, and prefers that which to be enjoyed must be given, to that which is bought.' The wise minister is concerned more with the permanent judgment of posterity than the superficial judgment of the contemporary mob. Being, like all wise men, a student of history, he 'considers his administration as a single day in the great year of government; but as a day that is affected by those which went before, and that must affect those which are to follow'.[35] Good government is for all time, and affects all time, even though it will itself in all probability disappear. Merely to consider the immediate gain is not fitting for the servants of the Patriot King. In thus summoning wise men to his council, the prince will be taking positive steps to ensure the effectiveness of his policies.

These steps, however, are not sufficient; the Patriot King must see that he does not become the prisoner of party, for even the wisest of his councillors may at times conspire together to gain results they deem best for society. The Patriot King will be outside party, for any party inevitably leads to faction. 'For faction is to party what the superlative is to the positive; party is a political evil, and faction is the worst of all parties.'[36] The ideal society exists when people and sovereign are united into one family, for in the family there are no parties. The king is the father of his people, the patriarch at the head and centre of the family, able to subdue by his good sense and true patriotism the factions which arise even in the best of families. A state of sweet reason and perfect harmony will be the result.

The Patriot King knows that 'all good ends of government' are most attainable in a united state.[37] However, this ideal union is not easily attained, since a people may wholeheartedly accept its prince but may not be united on particular measures proposed by various minority groups. The prince must then be the arbiter and check the balance of society by supporting for a time one group or another in order that the constitution and the government may survive. In so doing, however, he must always keep before him the vision of the free people unhampered in spirit and in action. It is the duty of all princes to know, warn and advise their subjects, but the Patriot King must also act on their behalf, since he is the perpetual chief minister, ever concerned with the past, present and future welfare of his people. 'He will defeat party in defense of the constitution . . . and lead men, from acting without party spirit, to act with national spirit.'[38]

If this were paradise, if man were without sin, and always acted under the tutelage of reason, the hopes and aspirations of prince and people would never be confounded. But, as man is imperfect, and as royal policies have to be administered by mortals, grievances will develop. Whether the grievances stem from acts of omission or commission is irrelevant; they are the results of human fallibility. And with grievances comes opposition. This opposition, however, need not be factious or wrong, since its origins may be legitimate, and there can be a loyal opposition, existing only until the grievances are removed. Any other form of opposition is bound to be partisan and factious, but under the reign of the Patriot King with his moral superiority, the lustre of his majesty and the purity of his government, this faction will make no progress. The evil prince, of course, will have none of these assets, with the result that conflicts may arise which will much diminish the royal power and may even cause the deposition and death of the king. In dealing with faction and with conflicts where the people lack unanimity, the good prince has many remedies at his disposal. He may identify himself with one group or another in the state, though he is not bound to them perpetually. What is more, the sovereign may use all his legitimate powers at hand to bring his works to fruition, for in so doing he is only aiding his people. As long as his motives are pure, he may even appear to succumb to party in order to restore the national unity lost through an imbalance in the state.

The fortunate sovereign is the one who has the complete submission of his people, and nothing more than disagreement over passing issues. If the disagreement is over the prince himself, his problems become vastly enlarged for, in order to gain his rights, he may have to use force to restore his subjects to a sense of their duty. If successful in this enterprise, he must not act as the conqueror but rather as the loving father who forgives his erring offspring, and by his character and influence command the immediate and lasting respect and affection of his subjects. True unity rather than military rule should be his aim. Naturally it is to be hoped that such extreme measures will never be necessary. Civil war which divides whole families is the cruellest of all conflicts, and it is the duty of the Patriot King to prevent this by uniting all families under his own universal patriarchy. Sometimes by devious and skilful arts a king can prevent the outbreak of such a conflict. By limiting the excessive enthusiasm of his partisans he may detach the more moderate of his opponents and so gain the necessary support. Moreover, some of his opponents may not really be against the sovereign himself, but rather against the court party which by its exuberant championship of the royal cause may have become as much a faction as his most ardent opponents. The limitation or curbing, therefore, of such supporters will help to conciliate the disaffected. The Patriot King becomes in consequence no longer a creature of party but the leader of all society. He becomes the leader of all primarily by upholding the law, because, although a man may oppose the king, he may not oppose the law; if the king upholds the constitution then he and the law are one. The sovereign should ever be mindful that his true aims are gained through national unity under the law, and they are not in the long term gained by the specious principle of *divide et impera*.

The Patriot King must do more than unite; he must also advance the welfare of the people, both by promoting spiritual values and by assisting material progress. However, the king must always guard against developments in material progress which tend to subvert the national character. Trade and commerce must be encouraged, taxes kept low and government expenditure reduced; government support should be given to the development of industry. At the same time there must be a concern for agriculture. It is significant that Bolingbroke was not tied to the interests of the landed classes, but recognised that a proper balance was as necessary in economics as in government. The Patriot King will also promote and support colonisation for colonies are 'so many farms of the mother country'.[39] Colonies are proper extensions of the parent state, not existing for themselves alone. They cannot be independent of the parent, but they are not inferior to the parent state since they are an integral part of the parent community.

Bolingbroke's reasons for advocating colonialism were frankly commercial, but he believed that, with unity and good government, both the colonists and the inhabitants of the parent state would prosper and that with prosperity would come happiness, to which each man has a right.

As a student of history, Bolingbroke, as we saw earlier, recognises the importance of the balance of power in international relations, and he recommends that the king adopt this as his guiding principle. If a proper balance of power is maintained, no one state can become dominant, and all are allowed to develop equally according to their talents. War as a policy is to be avoided, as it is expensive and wasteful, but the Patriot King will never be so pusillanimous as to invite attack from his more aggressive and unprincipled neighbours. The state with good natural frontiers is the most fortunate, but if his country lacks these, the prince will build adequate defences, for it is his first duty to protect his subjects. Bolingbroke's own national prejudices appear when he asserts that a navy is a better arm of defence than an army. A large army is too easily used to subvert the freedom of the people, and to maintain a large military force simply to demonstrate one's power is quite unnecessary and distinctly dangerous. The Patriot King will very wisely rid himself of such an encumbrance.

The Patriot King, then, will promote commerce and industry, defend his country and support true liberty, restore the national spirit and unite his people. In addition to these public policies he must be virtuous in his private life. The latter is almost as significant as his political duties, for he is ever on view. Royal failings must be hidden or disguised. All men have vices, but the 'virtues of the king' must not be 'lost in the vices of the man'. Taking Queen Elizabeth as the ruler most adept in combining public with private life, Bolingbroke says of her that in her private 'behaviour she showed great affability; she descended to familiarity; but her familiarity was such as could not be imputed to her weakness, and was, therefore, most justly ascribed to her goodness . . . She had private friendships, she had favourites; but she never suffered her friends to forget she was their queen; and when her favourites did, she made them feel that she was so.'[40] Other monarchs would be wise to be governed by such precepts. By behaving in the truly royal manner the sovereign will neither be despised nor hated. A king must be able to live as a private individual, but he must never forget that he is a sovereign, and this is part of the magic that he must maintain. He must say the right things and do the right things; ceremony is the public sign of his position, politeness is the private.

With his private life of so much significance, his private friends must conform to the standards set up for his official advisers. A double standard for kings is inadmissible. Bosom friends should not be those entrusted with authority; companions serve one purpose, councillors another; both are necessary to the ruler but each has its place. Weak kings have often lost power through entrusting it to favourites whose abilities they were quite incapable of assessing; friendship can make one blind to incompetence. History is scarred with the evil done by such men. Often unwitting in their viciousness, they were totally incapable of undertaking the tasks their royal masters permitted them to assume. Nestor playing the companion in folly is quite ridiculous, but even more so is the fool playing the Nestor. No sensible monarch will permit these rôles to be interchanged.

No king can truly assume the name of patriot if he allows any part of his court to dominate his life. Courtiers are playthings, they are ornaments to provide amusement and glamour, and should be nothing more. Male courtiers are dangerous, but female ones infinitely more so. The pleasures of feminine company are many, but in serious matters of state they should be absent. Too much feminine company is debilitating, and the sign of decadence. The court is an ever-present source of evil; the wise king will enjoy his courtiers, but will not rely upon them.

All that has been said is for the instruction of princes. The prince not yet in full possession of authority, if he but learn from the precepts given, will rule happily and well. Should the sovereign adopt the rôle designed for him by Bolingbroke, then the day of Plato's philosopher king will have arrived. His restoration will be the delight of his people and his reign counted great.

> What spectacle can be presented to the view of the mind so rare, so nearly divine, as a king possessed of absolute power, neither usurped by fraud, nor maintained by force, but by the genuine effect of esteem of confidence, and affection; the free gift of liberty, who finds her greatest security in this power, and would desire no other if the prince on the throne could be, what his people wish him to be, immortal? ... Concord will appear, brooding peace and prosperity on the happy land, joy sitting in every face, content in every heart; a people unoppressed, undisturbed, unalarmed; busy to improve their property and

the public stock; fleets covering the ocean, bringing home wealth by the returns of industry, carrying assistance or terror abroad by the direction of wisdom, and asserting triumphantly . . . right and . . . honour as far as waters roll and winds can waft them.[41]

A glorious picture is painted of the future, but this highly romanticised view of the sovereign was out of date even before Bolingbroke wrote. Events had already occurred which were to make his philosophy inapplicable. Kings in his sense could never more rule; they might reign, they might influence men, but the return to 'Good Queen Bess's golden days' was manifestly impossible. Probably Bolingbroke never expected such a restoration but only wished to portray an ideal: a state of liberty, an uncorrupted government, and a benign monarch. All of these were possible, but they were to arrive through a Patriot King of a different sort than the one he envisaged. The constitutional monarchy of the nineteenth and twentieth centuries which produced these conditions in his own country would be scarcely recognisable as a monarchy by Bolingbroke. If the prince has the virtues and esteem he desired, the direct political influence he presupposed has disappeared. If government is more stable and less corrupt, it is also dominated by the thing singled out for condemnation in *The Patriot King*—party. And in all but a few societies of today the very institution of monarchy has disappeared.

Yet, in many ways, the rôle he casts for the prince is one which is still highly relevant to republican constitutions in which the head of state has executive power and political initiative. And his ideas on the ends and methods of government and on the characteristics of a healthy political system have an important place in the political tradition of those contemporary societies whose aims are akin to those of *The Patriot King*: liberty, and the unity and harmony of the state.

7

Bolingbroke's Place
in the English Political
Tradition

This should have been a noble creature! He
Hath all the energy which would have made
A goodly frame of glorious elements,
Had they been wisely mingled; as it is,
It is an awful chaos—light and darkness,
And mind and dust, and passions and high thought,
Mixed and contending without end or order,
All dormant or destructive. He will perish.

BYRON

'WHO now reads Bolingbroke? Who ever read him
through?' Such was Edmund Burke's rather sarcastic
appraisal of the 'noble viscount' at the latter end of the
eighteenth century. Such an opinion of a man whose
name had once been magical and whose influence great, was perhaps
not surprising, for the world that he represented had passed away. The
heroes of England's Augustan age were now as much a part of the past
as were the heroes of the Carolean era. Inevitably the question must be
asked: did Bolingbroke have any lasting influence and did he leave any

political heirs? The answer is, no. At his death in 1752 the fickle public that had once been agog at his every act virtually disregarded him. It is true that when his collected works appeared in 1754 there was a great outcry, clerics fulminated against his theology, and juries were summoned to take action against the printer; but the reaction was only ephemeral, and Bolingbroke was soon forgotten.

He was not destined to be the founder of a great philosophical school; his writings were too much concerned with passing issues to be profound statements of eternal problems. Nor, indeed, did he have any immediate followers to continue his social theory and individualistic opportunism. Those who came after were cast in other moulds and seemed to think in different patterns. Perhaps, indeed, this is the essential characteristic of toryism: the absence of followers dedicated to a specific and defined political philosophy. It may be that it is inherently anti-tory to have a preconceived programme and that the true tory by definition is hostile, or at best indifferent, to such a concrete formulation. Toryism is a feeling; if it has a programme it is developed on a pragmatic basis and reflects current attitudes rather than an hypothetical utopia.

If Bolingbroke had disciples they were such only in the most general of ways. The Elder Pitt, for example, could be considered to have adopted one of the chief tenets of Bolingbroke in his detestation of party. But whereas Pitt probably held this belief in all sincerity, with Bolingbroke it was possibly a mere reaction against being denied power and office by the party politics of his own day. Whether he would have remained so opposed to party had he achieved political office is doubtful. Pitt's attitudes were expressed without prejudice, and when he returned to office in 1766 he set up a non-party ministry. The failure and incompetence of the Chatham Administration are well known. Perhaps it is unfair to damn non-party government on this example alone, but posterity is aware that England is unfavourable to coalitions. Non-party government was the figment of a creative imagination and certainly not the basis for action.

George III, to take another example, might be considered a disciple of Bolingbroke, and, indeed, was generally assumed to be so in the classic writings of the whig historians in the nineteenth century. There is no real indication that the king ever read Bolingbroke, and there is every sign that he was not the ideal Patriot King. Moreover 'the King's Friends' were not the men to eschew partisan politics; indeed, they were as factional as any political party. The Patriot King, therefore, was never destined to become a person but only to remain an ideal, as did Plato's philosopher kings. He does not seem possible—though Elizabeth I, Anne, and Victoria perhaps lend colour to the possibility of a Patriot Queen. A monarch who wields both distaff and sceptre seems more easily able to invoke a sense of chivalry, patriotism, and honour than a Patriot King.

Yet Burke's brusque rejection of Bolingbroke is rather unfair because it is quite clear that Bolingbroke played a considerable rôle in the development of Burke's thought and intellectual growth. Burke's earliest writing, *A Vindication of Natural Society* (1756), was a parody of Bolingbroke's views on 'natural religion'. So clever was the parody that many thought it a posthumous work of Bolingbroke's, and even when they learned to the contrary, they regarded Burke as an able young member of the rationalistic school. This Burke was never to be. Nor did he accept Bolingbroke's view that a king could rule without party. Custom, Burke held, was against it; the 'Constitutional Experiment' had proved the dangers inherent in such an idea; and he felt that the system as established was better than some newly contrived simple one. 'The nature of man is intricate; the objects of society are of the greatest possible complexity; and therefore the simple disposition or direction of power can be suitable either to man's nature or to the quality of his affairs. . . . The simple governments are fundamentally defective, to say no worse of them.'

Even so, Burke's attitude towards the past—and towards the Revolution of 1688 in particular—is very like Bolingbroke's own. Bolingbroke, the tory, shows whiggish traits in his opposition to the court faction, bribery, corruption and deceit. Burke, the 'old whig', is in the same tradition in making these his targets of opposition. Both men were consistent within their own traditions. Burke's gradual shift towards conservatism is part of his recognition of the values of the past, and in this also he resembles Bolingbroke who, though in his way a revolutionary, relied on certain immutable elements in the formation of history. Both of them, great haters and great spokesmen as they were, called on history to support them. Hence, for Burke to have said that he did not often quote Bolingbroke, nor did his works in general leave any permanent impression on his mind because 'he is a presumptuous and superficial writer' is, in many ways, a curious statement. He had obviously read Bolingbroke carefully, his style was a copy of Bolingbroke's own. But Burke had an odd turn of mind that may well have caused him to deny his obligations, even though these were limited, to one who had preceded him. Yet it is not so much that Burke was Bolingbroke's pupil, as that both had gained their ideas from the same teacher—history.

The most obvious disciple of Bolingbroke would seem to be Benjamin Disraeli. But to designate him as Bolingbroke's successor is to fail to understand the nature of Disraeli's conservatism. It is true that Disraeli with lavish language eulogised Bolingbroke as the creator of tory philosophy.* By Bolingbroke, according to Disraeli, the tories were released from their old dependence on Stuart doctrines of the seventeenth century, and given a liberalised modern philosophy based upon a popular national tradition. While this is true, much of Bolingbroke's philosophy in particular simply did not apply in the nineteenth century. Disraeli in fact used Bolingbroke, who was unread and whose name was virtually forgotten, as an eponymous sanction for his own personal reinterpretation of toryism.

Bolingbroke, despite his somewhat muddled epistomology, was a child of the newtonian age; Disraeli on the other hand was a romantic. He used the novel as the chief medium to expound his political ideas and his specifically political writings are insignificant. Disraeli saw life and society more through the eye and ear of the artist than through the mind of the conscious philosopher. There was also a streak of the egalitarian in him, although this arose from the fact that, being born a Jew in England, he was rather outside the classical social order of his own time. He also tended to outplay the English sense of honour by countering with the inherited values of the Sephardic Jew. Bolingbroke, on the contrary, was not an egalitarian, being convinced of the validity of the class system of his day. Indeed, there are no indications in his writings that he envisaged any widening of the franchise or any form of social democracy. Disraeli, therefore, either did not understand Bolingbroke or, alternatively, he deliberately misrepresented him. Furthermore, Disraeli did not differentiate between the tory party and the national party: for his purposes they were one and the same; whereas to Bolingbroke they were not, and in a sense it was only when he abandoned the partisanship of the tory party that he became the true spokesman of the national party.

Certainly both Bolingbroke and Disraeli were consciously involved with the past and with the stability of institutions and traditions anchored in the past. Neither of them was really concerned with

* See Appendix, p. 149.

abstract ideas; they wanted rather to see a revival of what they imagined
to be the old and pure English traditions.[1] They postulated a golden age,
set their myth in a historical context, and used it to sanction their
political pronouncements. They were concerned to present the thesis
that events and men are not isolated, but, when viewed from the
vantage point of history, are endowed with an organic unity. Their
aim was order not chaos, grace not vulgarity, and union not faction.

It is also possible to consider Winston Churchill in the tradition of
Bolingbroke. The former like the latter had a career in which he was
loved and hated by turns. His writings also look consciously to the past
with some considerable nostalgia, but at the same time they remind
successive generations that they are part of history and have a rôle to
play. For Churchill, as for Bolingbroke, history was not only the relics
of antiquity but also a guide for the future; it was indeed 'philosophy
teaching by examples'. Churchill, the Cassandra of the 1930s, was
fiercely critical of his opponents; but, unlike Bolingbroke, he did have
a new and greater time of power after his long sojourn in the wilder-
ness. Churchill's thesis was that of the true tory: the unity of society
and the greatness of the past; and in this he reflects the same tradition
in which Bolingbroke also stood.

Bolingbroke was also read outside England. On the continent he
found few followers; his style was admired but his ideas were incomprehensible or simply not applicable. The absolute monarchies and the
enlightened despotism were, to their adherents, obvious manifestations
of the Patriot King. The ideal had already been attained. In the New
World he was read widely, and leading Americans such as Jefferson,
Madison and Adams were all acquainted with his works; Madison and
Adams, and Washington too, all had distinct opinions on the dangers
of party,* but to what degree they were repeating what they may have
learned from Bolingbroke is an open question. It is true that Washington's conception of the position of the presidential office had much in
common with Bolingbroke's Patriot King, but again one must query
whether this was a consequence of the reading of Bolingbroke or the
spontaneous product of a high-minded and patriotic interpretation
of the duties of the head of a state.

From what has been said it is obvious that, except in the most general
fashion, Bolingbroke had no direct political heirs. It was impossible for
such a man to have successors. Nevertheless, he can still be regarded as

* Cf. *The Federalist Papers*, and also Washington's *Farewell Address*.

a true tory and a great tory philosopher, for great tories are not a recognisable part of the 'true blue' tradition. Indeed, it is the strange fate of the tories to be bound to leaders of uncongenial faith or suspicious antecedents. The great tory leaders have not necessarily even been tories throughout their careers. The Younger Pitt, claimed by the tories as one of their great inspirers, considered himself to be his father's political heir and a true whig. George Canning, who liberalised the tory party, was later to be repudiated by the old guard for his liberal policies. Wellington, superficially the *beau idéal* of toryism, was associated with some of the most radical measures of his day—Catholic Emancipation and the repeal of the Corn Laws—and by his calmness and rejection of the wiles of the ultras prevented a possible revolution in 1832. Robert Peel, who behaved like a liberal, thought like a liberal, and whose immediate followers in many cases became Liberals, was the leader of the old landed party until 1846. Benjamin Disraeli, who mixed orientalism and radicalism, who created Young England and Tory Democracy, was the idol of the tories in the conservative Victorian world. Winston Churchill, at first renegade Conservative, then Liberal cabinet minister, and later trenchant critic of the Conservative party, was yet in the end the symbol of his country and the mainstay of the party. It is tories such as these who are the great figures of the party. In comparison the Derbys, the Salisburys, the Bonar Laws, the Baldwins and the younger Chamberlains, are all respectable men, party men, rarely deviating from the accepted patterns and all good enough, but none of them can be considered creative or truly memorable figures.

There is no apostolic succession of toryism because the tory tradition is not that of consistency in ideology, but consistency in pragmatism. Politicians, after all, do not create ideas; and it is not the function of politicians as such to determine the immutable ends of human life, but only to assess the changing means by which ends generally accepted may best be attained. Ideas may alter, and a good tory will not hesitate to change his mind, for toryism is not bound to some particular thesis that restricts its course of action. Bolingbroke was part of this whole history. He was passionate, partisan and an opportunist. But in his endeavours to maintain the continuity of tory ideas of government while easing toryism out of its adherence to older formulations of its beliefs that were no longer applicable to changing circumstances, Bolingbroke prefigures the essential characteristics of the great tory leaders who came after him.

Appendix

Benjamin Disraeli on Lord Bolingbroke

(from THE VINDICATION OF THE BRITISH CONSTITUTION)

Gifted with that fiery imagination, the teeming fertility of whose inventive resources is as necessary to a great statesman or a great general as to a great poet; the ablest writer and the most accomplished orator of his age, that rare union in a country of free Parliaments and a free press insures to its possessor the privilege of exercising a constant influence over the mind of his country, that rare union that has rendered Burke so memorable; blending with that intuitive knowledge of his race, which creative minds alone can enjoy, all the wisdom which can be derived from literature, and a comprehensive experience of human affairs—no one was better qualified to be the Minister of a free and powerful nation than Henry St John; and Destiny at first appeared to combine with Nature in the elevation of his fortunes. Opposed to the Whigs from principle, for an oligarchy is hostile to genius, and recoiling from the Tory tenets, which his unprejudiced and vigorous mind taught him at the same time to dread and to contemn, Lord Bolingbroke, at the outset of his career, incurred the commonplace imputation of insincerity and inconsistency, because, in an age of unsettled parties with professions contradictory of their conduct, he maintained that vigilant and meditative independence which is the privilege of an original and determined spirit. It is probable that in the earlier years of his career he meditated over the formation of a new party, that dream of youthful ambition in a perplexed and discordant age, but destined in English politics to be never more substantial than a vision. More experienced in political life, he became aware that he had only to choose between the Whigs and the Tories, and his sagacious intellect, not satisfied with the superficial character of these celebrated divisions, penetrated their interior and essential qualities, and discovered, in spite of all the affectation of popular sympathy on one side, and of admiration of arbitrary power on the other, that the choice was in fact a choice between oligarchy and democracy. From the moment that Lord Bolingbroke, in becoming a Tory, embraced the national cause, he devoted himself absolutely to his party: all the energies of his Protean mind were lavished in their service; and although the ignoble prudence of the Whig Minister restrained him from advocating the cause of the nation in the senate, it was his inspiring pen that made Walpole tremble in the recesses of the Treasury, and in a series of writings, unequalled in our literature for their spirited patriotism, their just and profound views, and the golden eloquence in which they are expressed, eradicated from Toryism all those absurd and odious doctrines which Toryism had adventitiously adopted, clearly developed its essential and permanent character, discarded *jure divino*, demolished passive obedience, threw to the winds the doctrine of non-resistance, placed the abolition of James and the accession of George on their right basis, and in the complete reorganisation of the public mind laid the foundation for the future accession of the Tory party to power, and to that popular and triumphant career which must ever await the policy of an administration inspired by the spirit of our free and ancient institutions.

References

Bolingbroke's collected writings appeared in 1754 under the editorial supervision of Edward Mallet. The edition used here is that published in 1841 in Philadelphia: *The Works of Lord Bolingbroke, With a Life*, 4 vols. (The biographical section of this edition is a reprint of Oliver Goldsmith's *Life of Henry St John, Lord Viscount Bolingbroke*, first published in 1770.) The Philadelphia edition is hereinafter referred to as WORKS.

CHAPTER ONE

1. Oliver Goldsmith, 'The Life of Henry St John, Lord Viscount Bolingbroke' (London, 1770): see Introduction, WORKS, Vol. I, p. 13.
2. See introductory note above on sources.
3. Hassall, A., editor, *Lord Bolingbroke, Letters on the Spirit of Patriotism* (Oxford, 1917), p. xv.
4. Petrie, Charles, *Bolingbroke* (London, 1937), p. 17.
5. 'It puts me in mind of a Puritannical parson, Dr. Manton, who, if I mistake not—for I have never looked at the folio since I was a boy, and condemned sometimes to read in it—made a hundred and nineteen sermons on the CXIX psalm.' *Introduction to the Essay addressed to the Pope*, as quoted in Petrie, *op. cit.*, p. 16.
6. Walpole, H., *Memoirs of the Reign of George II* (London, 1846–47).
7. Swift, Jonathan, *Journal to Stella*, August 24, 1711.
8. *Edinburgh Review*, No. CXXVI, October 1863, p. 438.
9. For an account of Bolingbroke's matrimonial life see M. R. Hopkinson, *Married to Mercury* (London, 1936).
10. Quoted in Petrie, Charles, *op. cit.*, p. 47.
11. WORKS, Vol. II, p. 282.
12. Quoted in Douglas Harkness, *Bolingbroke, the Man and His Career* (London, 1957), p. 40.
13. WORKS, Vol. I, p. 115.
14. Macknight, Thomas, *The Life of Henry St. John, Viscount Bolingbroke* (London, 1863), p. 79.
15. Macknight, T., *op. cit.*, p. 85, and also Plumb, J. H., *Sir Robert Walpole: The Making of a Statesman* (London, 1956), p. 112.
16. Harkness, Douglas, *op. cit.*, p. 45.
17. WORKS, Vol. II, p. 295.
18. St John to Harley, November 6, 1708, *Harleian Mss. Collection: Bath Manuscripts*, Vol. I, p. 193.
19. WORKS, Vol. II, p. 345.

20. Macknight, Thomas, *op. cit.*, p. 127.
21. WORKS, Vol. II, pp. 344–45.
22. *National Review*, No. xxxii, April 1863, p. 395.
23. St John to Harley, October 11, 1708, *Harleian Mss. Collection: Bath Manuscripts*, Vol. I, p. 189.
24. WORKS, Vol. II, p. 8.
25. Macknight, Thomas, *op. cit.*, p. 151.
26. WORKS, Vol. I, pp. 114–15.
27. Oliver, F. S., *Endless Adventure* (London, 1930–35), Vol. I, p. 153.
28. Bolingbroke to Earl of Orrery, June 12, 1711; quoted in Macknight, Thomas, *op. cit.*, p. 201.
29. Macknight, Thomas, *op. cit.*, pp. 208–9.
30. Trevelyan, George M., *Two Party System in English Political History* (Oxford, 1926), p. 11.
31. WORKS, Vol. I, p. 115.
32. WORKS, Vol. II, pp. 430–31.
33. Churchill, W. S., *Marlborough* (New York, 1950), Vol. IV, p. 618.
34. Acton, Lord, *Home and Foreign Review*, Vol. II, April 1863, p. 635.
35. Petrie, Charles, *op. cit.*, p. 250.
36. Goldsmith, Oliver, *op. cit.*, in WORKS Vol. I, p. 70.
37. Robertson, Charles G., *Bolingbroke* (London, 1947), p. 8.
38. For a well-reasoned but contrary view see Plumb, J. H., *op. cit.*, pp. 213–14.
39. WORKS, Vol. I, pp. 112–13.
40. Macknight, Thomas, *op. cit.*, p. 488.
41. *Ibid.*, p. 489.
42. *Ibid.*, p. 534.
43. Petrie, Charles, *op. cit.*, p. 299.
44. For an excellent account of the negotiations and their outcome, see Plumb, J. H., *Sir Robert Walpole: The King's Minister* (London, 1960), pp. 124–27.
45. WORKS, Vol. II, pp. 369–70.
46. For an account of Bolingbroke's activities at this time, see Archibald S. Foord, *His Majesty's Opposition* (Oxford, 1964), pp. 113–216.
47. Goldsmith, Oliver, *op. cit.*, in WORKS, Vol. I, p. 112.
48. Hassall, A., *Bolingbroke* (Oxford, 1915), p. 208.
49. Trevelyan, G. M., *op. cit.*, p. 20.
50. *National Review*, No. xxxii, April 1863, p. 426.

CHAPTER TWO
1. Becker, Carl, *Every Man His Own Historian* (New York, 1935).
2. Goldsmith, Oliver, *op. cit.*, in WORKS, p. 112.
3. WORKS, Vol. II, p. 174.
4. *Ibid.*, p. 175.
5. *Ibid.*, p. 175.
6. *Ibid.*, p. 177.
7. Collingwood, R. G., *The Idea of History* (Oxford, 1940), p. 10.
8. *Ibid.*

9. Pope, A., *Essay on Man*, Epistle IV, lines 363–68.
10. WORKS, Vol. II, p. 179.
11. *Ibid.*, p. 194.
12. *Ibid.*, p. 186.
13. *Ibid.*, p. 179.
14. *Ibid.*, p. 186.
15. *Ibid.*, p. 185.
16. *Ibid.*, p. 185.
17. *Ibid.*, p. 185.
18. *Ibid.*, p. 186.
19. Becker, Carl, *op. cit.*, pp. 120–21.
20. Joseph H. W., *An Introduction to Logic* (Oxford, 1916), p. 492.
21. WORKS, Vol. II, p. 191.
22. *Ibid.*, p. 191 and p. 192 *passim*.
23. *Ibid.*, p. 193.
24. *Ibid.*, p. 193.
25. *Ibid.*, p. 194.
26. *Ibid.*, p. 190.
27. *Ibid.*, p. 191.
28. *Ibid.*, p. 201.
29. *Ibid.*, p. 201.
30. *Ibid.*, p. 203.
31. *Ibid.*, p. 204.
32. *Ibid.*, p. 205.
33. *Ibid.*, p. 206.
34. *Ibid.*, p. 207.
35. *Ibid.*, p. 211.
36. *Ibid.*, p. 212.
37. *Ibid.*, p. 212.
38. *Ibid.*, p. 212.
39. *Ibid.*, p. 212.
40. *Ibid.*, p. 213.
41. *Ibid.*, p. 217.
42. *Ibid.*, p. 223.
43. *Ibid.*, p. 226.
44. *Ibid.*, p. 227.
45. *Ibid.*, p. 239.
46. Trevelyan, George M., *Bolingbroke on the Study and Use of History*, 'Introduction', p. x.
47. WORKS, Vol. I, p. 502.
48. WORKS, Vol. II, p. 248.
49. WORKS, Vol. I, p. 332.
50. *Ibid.*, p. 368.
51. *Ibid.*, p. 386.
52. *Ibid.*, p. 385.
53. WORKS, Vol. II, p. 240.
54. *Ibid.*, p. 241.
55. WORKS, Vol. I, p. 396.

56. WORKS, Vol. II, pp. 229–30.

CHAPTER THREE

1. For a very full treatment of Bolingbroke's views on religion see Walter M. Merrill, *From Statesman to Philosopher: A Study in Bolingbroke's Deism* (New York, 1949).
2. Blake, William, 'To the Deists', in *Jerusalem*.
3. WORKS, Vol. II, p. 466.
4. *Ibid.*, p. 466.
5. WORKS, Vol. III, p. 33.
6. WORKS, Vol. II, p. 465.
7. *Ibid.*, p. 463.
8. *Ibid.*, p. 463.
9. Thomas Aquinas, *Summa Contra Gentiles*, IV, i.
10. WORKS, Vol. IV, p. 251.
11. As quoted in an unpublished 'critical note' by Gerald Bostock.
12. WORKS, Vol. III, p. 34.
13. *Ibid.*, p. 34.
14. *Ibid.*, p. 34.
15. *Ibid.*, p. 34.
16. WORKS, Vol. II, pp. 503–4.
17. WORKS, Vol. III, pp. 32–33.
18. *Ibid.*, p. 39.
19. *Ibid.*, p. 36.
20. *Ibid.*, p. 37.
21. Cooke, George W., *Memoirs of Lord Bolingbroke* (London, 1836–37), Vol. II, p. 121.
22. WORKS, Vol. III, p. 396, and Vol. IV, p. 109.
23. WORKS, Vol. III, p. 396.
24. *Ibid.*, p. 420.
25. *Ibid.*, p. 422.
26. *Ibid.*, p. 423.
27. *Ibid.*, p. 426.
28. *Ibid.*, p. 427.
29. *Ibid.*, p. 428.
30. *Ibid.*, p. 429.
31. *Ibid.*, p. 435.
32. *Ibid.*, p. 436.
33. *Ibid.*, p. 437.
34. *Ibid.*, p. 442.
35. *Ibid.*, p. 442.
36. *Ibid.*, p. 447.
37. *Ibid.*, p. 457.
38. WORKS, Vol. II, p. 508.
39. WORKS, Vol. III, p. 186.
40. WORKS, Vol. IV, pp. 335–36.
41. *Ibid.*, pp. 428–29.
42. Pope, Alexander, *Essay on Man*, Epistle IV, lines 394–98.

43. Blake, William, 'The Clod and the Pebble'.

CHAPTER FOUR

1. Aristotle, *Nichomachean Ethics*, Bk. I, Chapter VII; quoted in Richard McKeon, *Introduction to Aristotle* (New York, 1947), p. 317.
2. WORKS, Vol. IV, p. 182.
3. *Ibid.*, p. 189.
4. *Ibid.*, p. 190.
5. Seneca, *De Clementia*, I, 4.
6. WORKS, Vol. IV, p. 191.
7. *Corinthians II*, Chapter V, verse 10.
8. WORKS, Vol. IV, p. 193.
9. *Ibid.*, p. 194.
10. *Ibid.*, p. 195.
11. Locke, John, *Civil Government*, Chapter VIII; as quoted in Bolingbroke, WORKS, Vol. IV, p. 195.
12. WORKS, Vol. IV, pp. 195–96.
13. *Ibid.*, p. 196.
14. *Ibid.*, p. 196.
15. *Ibid.*, p. 199.
16. Aristotle, *Nichomachean Ethics*, Bk. I, Chapter VII; McKeon, *op. cit.*, p. 317.
17. WORKS, Vol. II, p. 81.
18. *Ibid.*, p. 88.
19. *Ibid.*, p. 381.
20. *Ibid.*, p. 85.
21. *Ibid.*, p. 85.
22. *Ibid.*, p. 87.
23. *Ibid.*, p. 117.
24. *Ibid.*, p. 118.
25. *Ibid.*, p. 118.
26. *Ibid.*, p. 150.
27. *Ibid.*, p. 119.
28. *Ibid.*, p. 119.
29. *Ibid.*, p. 119.
30. *Ibid.*, pp. 119–20.
31. *Ibid.*, p. 120.
32. *Ibid.*, p. 120.
33. *Ibid.*, p. 101.
34. *Ibid.*, p. 102.
35. *Ibid.*, p. 106.
36. *Ibid.*, p. 127.
37. *Ibid.*, p. 148.
38. *Ibid.*, p. 91.
39. *Ibid.*, p. 150.
40. *Ibid.*, p. 112.

CHAPTER FIVE

1. WORKS, Vol. II, pp. 23–24.

2. WORKS, Vol. II, p. 24.
3. *Ibid.*, p. 24.
4. *Ibid.*, p. 27.
5. *Ibid.*, p. 27.
6. *Ibid.*, p. 27.
7. *Ibid.*, pp. 27–28.
8. *Ibid.*, p. 30.
9. *Ibid.*, p. 30.
10. *Ibid.*, pp. 32–33.
11. *Ibid.*, p. 35.
12. *Ibid.*, pp. 36–37.
13. *Ibid.*, p. 39.
14. *Ibid.*, p. 46.
15. *Ibid.*, pp. 47–48.
16. *Ibid.*, p. 48.
17. *Ibid.*, p. 54.
18. *Ibid.*, p. 57.
19. *Ibid.*, p. 61.
20. *Ibid.*, p. 63.
21. *Ibid.*, p. 64 and p. 66.
22. *Ibid.*, p. 70.
23. *Ibid.*, p. 71.
24. *Ibid.*, p. 74.
25. *Ibid.*, p. 75.
26. *Ibid.*, p. 76.
27. *Ibid.*, p. 79.
28. *Ibid.*, p. 435.
29. *Ibid.*, p. 435.
30. *Ibid.*, p. 435.
31. *Ibid.*, p. 290.
32. *Ibid.*, p. 313.
33. *Ibid.*, p. 433.
34. WORKS, Vol. I, p. 114.
35. *Ibid.*, p. 115.
36. *Ibid.*, p. 121.
37. WORKS, Vol. II, p. 434.
38. *Ibid.*, p. 436.
39. WORKS, Vol. I, p. 128.
40. *Ibid.*, p. 131.
41. WORKS, Vol. II, pp. 86–87.
42. *Ibid.*, p. 93.
43. *Ibid.*, p. 93.
44. *Ibid.*, p. 94.
45. *Ibid.*, p. 94.
46. *Ibid.*, p. 94.
47. *Ibid.*, p. 162.
48. *Ibid.*, pp. 369–70.
49. *Ibid.*, p. 171.

50. WORKS, Vol. II, p. 438.

CHAPTER SIX

1. For varying views on Prince Frederick, see: Lord Hervey, *Memoirs* (London, 1931); Horace Walpole, *Memoires of the Reign of George II* (London, 1846–47); Sir George Young, *Poor Fred: The People's Prince* (London, 1937); and Averyl Edwards, *Frederick Louis, Prince of Wales, 1707–51* (London, 1947).
2. WORKS, Vol. II, p. 374.
3. *Ibid.*, p. 375.
4. *Ibid.*, p. 377.
5. *Ibid.*, p. 378.
6. *Ibid.*, p. 379.
7. *Ibid.*, p. 379.
8. *Ibid.*, pp. 379–80.
9. *Ibid.*, p. 380.
10. *Ibid.*, p. 380.
11. *Ibid.*, pp. 380–81.
12. *Ibid.*, p. 383.
13. *Ibid.*, p. 382.
14. *Ibid.*, p. 382.
15. *Ibid.*, p. 382.
16. *Ibid.*, p. 380.
17. *Ibid.*, p. 384.
18. *Ibid.*, p. 384.
19. *Ibid.*, p. 386.
20. *Ibid.*, p. 388.
21. *Ibid.*, p. 390.
22. *Ibid.*, pp. 391–92.
23. *Ibid.*, p. 392.
24. *Ibid.*, p. 392.
25. *Ibid.*, p. 393.
26. *Ibid.*, p. 393.
27. *Ibid.*, p. 395.
28. *Ibid.*, p. 396.
29. *Ibid.*, pp. 396–97.
30. *Ibid.*, p. 397.
31. *Ibid.*, p. 397.
32. *Ibid.*, p. 399.
33. *Ibid.*, p. 400.
34. *Ibid.*, p. 400.
35. *Ibid.*, p. 401.
36. *Ibid.*, p. 401.
37. *Ibid.*, p. 402.
38. *Ibid.*, p. 403.
39. *Ibid.*, p. 416.
40. *Ibid.*, pp. 421–25, *passim.*
41. *Ibid.*, pp. 428–29.

CHAPTER SEVEN

1. For a modern view of this see Richard Faber, *Beaconsfield and Bolingbroke* (London, 1961), pp. 73–91.

Select Bibliography

Becker, Carl, *Every Man His Own Historian* (New York, 1935)

Bolingbroke, Viscount, *The Works of Lord Bolingbroke With a Life* (Philadelphia, 1841)

Churchill, Winston, *Marlborough: His Life and Times* (London, 1933–38)

Clark, G. N., *The Later Stuarts 1660–1714* (Oxford, 1949)

Collingwood, R. G., *The Idea of History* (Oxford, 1946)

Collins, John C., *Bolingbroke a Historical Study; and Voltaire in England* (New York, 1886)

Cooke, George W., *The History of a Party . . . 1666–1832* (London, 1836–37)

Cooke, George W., *Memoirs of Lord Bolingbroke* (London, 1836)

Disraeli, Benjamin (Lord Beaconsfield), *The Works &c.* (London, 1904)

Edwards, Averyl, *Frederick Louis Prince of Wales 1707–1751* (London, 1947)

Faber, Richard, *Beaconsfield and Bolingbroke* (London, 1961)

Feiling, Keith, *History of the Tory Party 1640–1714* (Oxford, 1924)

Feiling, Keith, *The Second Tory Party 1714–1832* (Oxford, 1938)

Foord, Archibald S., *His Majesty's Opposition* (Oxford, 1964)

Goldsmith, Oliver, *The Life of Henry St John, Lord Viscount Bolingbroke* (London, 1770)

Harkness, Douglas, *Bolingbroke, the Man and his Career* (London, 1957)

Harrop, R., *Bolingbroke, a Political Study and Criticism* (London, 1884)

Hassall, A., *Life of Viscount Bolingbroke* (Oxford, 1915)

Hassall, A. (ed.), *Lord Bolingbroke, Letters on the Spirit of Patriotism* (Oxford, 1917)

Hopkinson, M. R., *Married to Mercury* (London, 1936)

James, D. G., *The Life of Reason* (London, 1949)

Joseph, Horace W., *An Introduction to Logic* (Oxford, 1916)

Macknight, Thomas, *Life of Henry St John, Viscount Bolingbroke* (London, 1863)

Merrill, Walter M., *From Statesman to Philosopher: A Study in Bolingbroke's Deism* (New York, 1949)

Michael, Wolfgang, *England Under George I. The Beginnings of the Hanoverian Dynasty* (London, 1936)

Oliver, F. S., *Endless Adventure* (London, 1930–35)

Pares, Richard, *Limited Monarchy in Great Britain in the Eighteenth Century* (London, 1957)

Parke, Gilbert, editor, *Letters and Correspondence, Public and Private, of the Right Hon. Henry St John, Lord Viscount Bolingbroke* (London, 1798)

Petrie, Charles, *Bolingbroke* (London, 1937)

Plumb, J. H., *Sir Robert Walpole: The Making of a Statesman* (London, 1956)

Plumb, J. H., *Sir Robert Walpole: The King's Minister* (London, 1960)

Robertson, Charles G., *Bolingbroke* (London, 1947)

Sichel, Walter, *Bolingbroke and his Times* (London, 1901)

Swift, Jonathan, *Works* (London, 1883–84)
Trevelyan, G. M., *Bolingbroke's Defence of the Treaty of Utrecht &c.* (Cambridge, 1932)
Trevelyan, G. M., *England under Queen Anne* (London, 1930–34)
Trevelyan, G. M., *England under the Stuarts* (London, 1946–47)
Trevelyan, G. M., *Two Party System in English Political History* (Oxford, 1926)
Walpole, Horace, *Memoires of the Reign of George II* (London, 1846–47)

Index

DATE DUE

JA 5 '68			
NO 30 '67			
MR 27 '69			
GAYLORD			PRINTED IN U.S.A.